How to Increase Giving in Your Church

George Barna

How to Increase Giving in Your Church

George Barna

Regal

A Division of Gospel Light
Ventura, California, U.S.A.

Published by Regal Books
From Gospel Light
Ventura, California, U.S.A.
Printed in the U.S.A.

Cover Design by Barbara LeVan Fisher
Interior Design by Britt Rocchio
Edited by Virginia Woodard

Library of Congress Cataloging-in-Publication Data
Barna, George.
    How to increase giving in your church / George Barna.
      p. cm.
    Includes bibliographical references.
    ISBN 0-8307-1921-0 (trade paper)
    1. Church fund raising. I. Title.
    BV772.5.B36 1997   97-3212
    254'.8—dc21   CIP

4 5 6 7 8 9 10 11 12 13 14 15 16 17 18 19 20 21 22 23 24 25 / 06 05 04 03 02

Rights for publishing this book in other languages are contracted by Gospel Light Worldwide, the
international nonprofit ministry of Gospel Light. Gospel Light Worldwide also provides publishing
and technical assistance to international publishers dedicated to producing Sunday School and
Vacation Bible School curricula and books in the languages of the world. For additional information, visit
www.gospellightworldwide.org; write to Gospel Light Worldwide, P.O. Box 3875, Ventura, CA 93006;
or send an e-mail to info@gospellightworldwide.org.

Contents

One of Americans' distinctives is our willingness to give
away large sums of money to charitable organizations
and to churches.

Americans are the most generous people in the world,
but giving is generally on the decline, and the amounts
given vary by age segments of the population.

The myths and truths about giving are surprising.
Americans tend to see everything as related to everything else.

Church donors can be evaluated in terms of demographics (personal background), psychographics (attitudes and values) and theolographics™ (spiritual perspectives and practices).

People no longer give to the church simply because it is
the church. The church must prove it is worthy of donations through the mark it leaves on the world.

God's Word consistently and boldly speaks to the issue
of stewardship. Congregations need to be informed by a
simple strategy: "Preach the Word."

Appendices

Acknowledgments

I am grateful to the many people who have helped make this book possible. Here are a few of those individuals.

My ministry partners at Regal Books have been supportive, as usual. Among the people with whom I have had contact on this project are Bill Greig III, Bill Greig Jr., Kyle Duncan, Bill Denzel, Cary Maxon, Gloria Moss and Virginia Woodard. I gratefully acknowledge the efforts of the dozens of "behind-the-scenes" people who labored to make this manuscript a ministry resource for many.

My ministry partners at Barna Research held the company together during my periods of isolation to write this book. Deserving special merit for their tenacity—or was it enjoyment?—of my absences are David Kinnaman, Jill Kinnaman and Pam Tucker.

My thanks are due to the thousands of pastors, church leaders and adults across America whom we interviewed for the research described in this book. Without their insights I would have had very little to say. I hope this book captures their perspectives and experiences accurately, and in a way which enables them to advance the cause of Christ.

My most special thanks, as always, go to my family. My wife, Nancy, gets the most credit of anyone for the completion of this book. This is the most difficult book I have ever written, but she has been unwavering in her support of my calling to provide the Church with information that will lead to better strategic decisions for ministry. She filled the vacuum in our family created by my absence to write. Naturally, my daughters, Samantha and Corban, have been affected by those gaps in our growing relationship, but have also been nothing less than affirming of this adventure.

May God pour a special blessing upon these people for the sacrifices they have made, and for the blessings they have bestowed upon me. May this book be a blessing to Him and His people.

Introduction

Americans are different from adults in other developed nations of the world. We are the more likely to sue our fellow citizens. Despite our glorious national history, we are comparatively ill-informed about it. Compared to people in other developed nations, we are more comfortable living with debt, and less comfortable living with relatives. We treasure pleasure, yet we are comparative workaholics. We are more keenly devoted to the television set. Americans consume pizza as if it were a miracle drug. We are more likely to abort our babies and divorce our spouses. We attend church more often than do our peers in other first-world nations. We set the pace when it comes to transforming entertainers—athletes, singers, TV and movie performers—into wealthy, pampered cultural icons.

One of the most striking distinctives, though, is our willingness to give away large sums of money to organizations whose sole purpose is to enhance people's quality of life—usually *other* people's quality of life. To facilitate this focus, we have created an entire sector of the national economy known as the nonprofit sector. It encompasses more than a million organizations (churches included). These organizations have combined assets estimated at more than $850 billion, evidence that the good-deeds business has grown way beyond "mom-and-pop" status within our national economy.[1]

Americans warmly embrace these service-minded entities, as witnessed by the dramatic revenue rise experienced by nonprofits during the past quarter of the twentieth century. In 1970, the AAFRC Trust for Philanthropy reported that philanthropic giving by individuals reached $16 billion. Its figures for 1995 indicate that individual gifts exceeded $120 billion.[2] That is more than a sevenfold increase in just 25 years. From 1970 through 1995, our population increased by just 30 percent—so the increased levels of giving cannot be attributed solely to our expanding population.

Even when compared to other economic measures during the past two decades, giving has increased at a faster pace. Although giving by individuals jumped by 556 percent, America's gross domestic product (GDP) increased by

461 percent, the personal income of Americans rose by 482 percent and personal consumption expenditures grew by 404 percent.[3] In other words, people's determination to give away their money to those in need is a remarkable story. The inclination to demonstrate compassion toward humanity may be one of the paradoxes of a society widely known for its selfishness and self-indulgence, but it is a reality that cannot be denied.

> **"NO PERSON WAS EVER HONORED FOR WHAT HE RECEIVED. HONOR HAS BEEN THE REWARD FOR WHAT HE GAVE." CALVIN COOLIDGE**

If you need further evidence of the significance of the nonprofit sector to the national economy, or to understand just how integral the sector is to the nation's economic and moral fabric, realize that more than 7 million people are employed by such organizations. That is 1 out of every 17 people in the labor force. These organizations have a cumulative annual operating budget of nearly $400 billion; and the economic activities of nonprofit entities account for 7 percent of the nation's gross national product (GNP).[4]

The initial recipients of the public's willful generosity (i.e., the nonprofit organizations) have become experts at marketing to people's interest in facilitating the well-being of society. Some nonprofit organizations—including, but certainly not limited to, churches and religious organizations—teach people of the personal benefits, both now and eternally, of sharing their financial resources with those who are in need. Other nonprofit organizations have developed elaborate and sophisticated fund-raising and promotional campaigns that raise substantial sums of money. This is attributable to the ability to strategically market services that fulfill people's felt needs to help other people or to make a difference in the world.

The kinds of organizations that raise money for good works are a fascinating study in specialization and diversity. Nonprofit organizations include those involved in work related to health care, medical research, disaster relief, education, public welfare, the arts, religion, legal protection, community development and more. The landscape of nonprofit organizations ranges from multibillion dollar giants employing staffs of thousands of people and center-city offices in cities across the world to tiny volunteer-based neighborhood organizations operating out of a basement or garage. Some nonprofit organizations have become household names: United Way, Salvation Army, American Cancer Society, American Red Cross and the YMCA are just a few examples.

Literally thousands of these charitable entities were begun in the United States and have since spread throughout the world. They are doing good deeds for those in need outside the United States as well as generating revenue and other forms of assistance from warmhearted people around the globe. Of all the exports the United States can claim, perhaps we should be most proud of the charitable organizations and activities conceived, funded and implemented by Americans and the agencies we birthed for this purpose.

Widespread Personal Involvement

The end result is that millions of Americans think of donating to charity as a personal social obligation. Sociologists inform us that we are living in an era in which American society reinvents itself on a three-to-five year cycle. We thereby radically and rapidly reshape many of the fundamental attitudes, values and behaviors that direct our daily existence. Americans' tendency to give money to nonprofit organizations, however, has remained one of the comparatively few constants in the midst of a changing, unpredictable culture.

Providing tangible support for nonprofit enterprises is not simply the altruistic whim of a small proportion of households that live in relative affluence. About three out of every four households in this country contribute money to nonprofit organizations they deem reputable and worthy. A majority of the population gives money to churches and religious groups; millions of adults also give money to nonreligious causes and groups. Such commitment and behavior says much about the character, traditions and worldview of the American people.

Reflecting the values of the nation—as a representative, democratic form of government theoretically does—even the laws of our federal and state governments provide rewards and incentives to those who choose to help others through their charitable donations. Nonprofit organizations also benefit from special laws that protect their ability to do their work, unfettered by many of the regulatory hassles to which for-profit organizations are subjected. One of the most valuable benefits nonprofits receive is the ability to own land without paying property tax. This alone saves the nonprofit industry billions of dollars of revenue every year.

Furthering Religious Efforts

In spite of the fact that most people are involved in charitable giving, many of the people I speak with are surprised to learn that of all the various kinds of work donors support, by far the best-funded segment of the nonprofit community is the religious segment. Simply put, more people give to religious organizations than to any other kind; more gifts are given to religious organizations; and the greatest amount of money is given to faith entities. Giving to religious organizations is the most common kind of giving in the United States.

Giving to Support Churches

The best-funded segment of the best-funded category of nonprofits (i.e., religious entities) is churches. The 300,000-plus churches in the United States are all donor supported. When we examine the funds raised by denominational churches each year, the sums are staggering. If we aggregate the money raised by churches within each of the 200-plus denominations ministering in the United States, at least six denominations' member churches cumulatively raised more than $1 billion in 1995.

The billion-dollar denominations were the Southern Baptist Convention, Roman Catholic Church, United Methodist Church, Presbyterian Church (U.S.A.), Episcopal Church and the Evangelical Lutheran Church in America. Several other denominations each brought in somewhere between $250 million and $1 billion, including the Lutheran Church—Missouri Synod, Presbyterian Church in America, United Church of Christ, Seventh-day Adventists, Christian Church (Disciples of Christ), Church of the Nazarene, Salvation Army and the American Baptist Church.[5]

In spite of these almost-unfathomable sums, most church leaders dislike talking about the need for money to facilitate church-based ministry. Like it or not, the reality is that leading a church to an effective ministry requires money. As a result, those of us involved in leadership within a church must be knowledgeable and wise about fund-raising.

> "IF A PERSON GETS HIS ATTITUDE TOWARD MONEY STRAIGHT, IT WILL HELP STRAIGHTEN OUT ALMOST EVERY OTHER AREA IN HIS LIFE."
> BILLY GRAHAM

I know, based on research results and on personal experience, that most ministers are not focused on money and have a rather healthy disinterest in (if not a strong distaste for) financial matters. One of the reasons some outsiders perceive churches to be "money hungry" is that most of us are ill at ease when it comes to thinking, talking about and handling money matters.

The folks in the pews are used to professional presentations from us—

whether those be in the form of sermons, training lectures or formal class-room instruction. When it comes to presentations regarding the church's need for bucks, though, we become transformed people—and not for the better! Most pastors, church staff and lay leaders are both inadequately trained and emotionally unprepared for communicating about and actually raising the kind of money required to lead a church toward the fulfillment of its vision. Often—too often, perhaps—our lack of preparation shows.

The Thrust of This Book

One of the fundamental shifts redefining the new America has been the increasing significance of information in marketing and management prac-tices. These days, only the most adventurous—or foolhardy—large organi-zations would dare to make major corporate decisions regarding strategy and tactics without first scrutinizing crucial data about the market. Even in the nonprofit arena, which has traditionally lagged noticeably behind the for-profit sector in its professional development and sophistication, the value of targeted information in decision making has become much more important and high profile in the past decade.

This book is geared toward helping church leaders acquire current and accurate knowledge about the who, how and why of giving to churches. In the pages that follow, I want to address some basic questions about the givers (their demographics, psychographics, theolographics) and their giv-ing (why do they give, how do they give, how much do they give, what would encourage them to give more). This information may help diffuse some of the most common sources of anxiety, fear and misunderstanding related to fund-raising. Although I cannot offer any magic formulas or fool-proof gimmicks, you will receive insight into some fundamental truths you need to know about people and their financial giving if you wish to raise money for your church's activities.

The basis of these insights is research conducted during the past four years by the Barna Research Group, a marketing research company that has been studying ministries and donors for more than a decade. The informa-tion contained in this book is drawn from 11 large-scale, nationwide, non-proprietary studies conducted by Barna Research from July 1992 through August 1996.

The information and conclusions provided in this report are based on extensive personal interviews conducted by my company with more than 10,000 adults randomly selected from across the nation. Most of those peo-ple reported they were donors to nonprofit organizations, but we also gleaned information from several thousand adults who do not contribute to any churches or nonprofit organizations.

In preparing to write this book, I examined the information from four key segments of people: those who donate to churches, only; those who donate to nonprofit organizations, but not to churches; those who donate both to churches and nonchurch nonprofits; and those who donate to neither churches nor nonprofits. By including all four segments in my analysis, I have gained a richer context for understanding donor psychology and behavior. Although my focus will be upon those who donate to churches, my overall understanding and base of conclusions have been formed by a broader body of insights gained from this macrolevel evaluation.

Through the Barna Research Group, I began studying the donor-church relationship more than a decade ago. The impetus was a conviction that for churches and their donors to optimize their relationship, each needed to have accurate and useful information about the other party. Donors, of course, have no legal obligation to support churches. Their donations are indicative of a personal desire to do what they believe is right, whether that conviction is based on a sense of moral obligation, biblical responsibility, ego or emotional need. Concurrently, every church has a responsibility to understand the motivations of the donor and to respond in an informed, ethical and purposeful manner. Such a response cannot be implemented until sufficient knowledge of the donor is gained to stimulate positive, substantive interaction. That response means more than simply demonstrating the ability to solicit greater amounts of funding from the donor.

In the for-profit business world, the bottom line is net profit. In the church world, the bottom line is the quality and quantity of authentic ministry (i.e., life transformation) facilitated by people's contributions. Given this reality, in church fund-raising each party has a serious responsibility to the other: It is never to be a situation in which the donor is responsible to give and the church is responsible to take without significant reciprocation.

An Opportunity for Leadership

Naturally, no report or research study can tell you what to do. Your context for ministry is unique, and brainlessly implementing a generic strategy from a how-to manual will not produce the kind of results your ministry needs—or deserves. The information in this book can, however, identify high-potential opportunities or likely barriers to optimal performance. Ultimately, it is my desire that this information will help you to position stewardship within your church's ministry for maximum effect.

By understanding people's motivations, their inclinations and how to communicate more effectively with them, it will be possible to break through barriers that might otherwise remain impenetrable. Use these insights to spark new ideas, to refine existing programs and perspectives, and to avoid unnecessary mistakes and difficulties.

Come now and join me on a journey through the thought processes, values, beliefs and lifestyles that lead nearly 100 million adults every year to ante up and intentionally help those who cannot adequately help themselves.

Notes

1. See *Nonprofit Alert* (June 1993): 1.
2. *Giving USA* (New York: AAFRC Trust for Philanthropy, 1992).
3. U.S. Bureau of the Census, *Statistical Abstract of the United States, 1992* (Washington, D.C.: U.S.G.P.O., 1992), tables 1, 673, 681, 682.
4. Data from the Chronicle of Philanthropy promotional mailing, 1993.
5. Kenneth Bedell, ed., *Yearbook of American and Canadian Churches* (Nashville: Abingdon Press, 1996), pp. 274-277.

1

A Reality Check

"**THINK OF GIVING NOT AS A DUTY**

BUT AS A PRIVILEGE."

JOHN D. ROCKEFELLER JR.

Jack Ellis is the founder and CEO of a nonprofit organization whose primary purpose is distributing evangelistic literature throughout the English-speaking world.[1] He is absolutely committed to the task of evangelism, and has personally led hundreds of people to Christ. During his 20-plus years in full-time parachurch ministry, he has seen his organization ride the funding roller coaster. He had some robust years financially and some years during which he was ready to declare bankruptcy. Jack will tell you that doing ministry is what makes his life fulfilling; raising the money to do ministry is what makes it agonizing.

As we sat down for lunch one afternoon to catch up on what was happening in our respective lives and ministries, he repeated a comment he had been making occasionally in jest for several years, but which now had become his mantra. "If only God provided the money for His work we could get the job of world evangelization done."

Not long after that I had an occasion to speak about ministry and money at a conference for pastors. It was an ecumenical setting attended by pastors from more than 25 denominations, and who came from every state in the union. After the presentation, I was surrounded by a group of pastors who wanted to discuss some of the ideas to which they had been exposed. One of the people who approached me with a question was a denominational executive. He works with more than 1,000 churches nationwide, helping them with financial management and fund-raising. After I addressed his specific question, his parting comment to me gave me a sense of deja vu: "Well, George, I cannot disagree that the world is changing quickly and we have to adapt to the new ministry environment. But I still don't see how we can be so flexible and adaptive if people won't contribute enough money to allow us to minister effectively."

Probably no more than a month later I spoke at another conference attended by pastors. On that occasion, I was addressing research I had conducted about stewardship practices in churches. Just before we began a question-and-answer session following my presentation, I quickly reviewed the index cards on which audience members had written their questions. One of the most frequently submitted questions was the following: How can we grow the Church when God's people are giving less of their money for the work of the Church? One pastor put a different spin on the question: Is there really enough money available today to complete the tasks given to us in Scripture? Still another pastor raised the same issue from yet another angle: Do you suppose that perhaps God is seeking to limit our personal ambitions in ministry by limiting the cash we have access to for pursuing our ministry dreams?

Deep down I feel some discomfort at even addressing the question of whether the Church has the money it needs to do God's work. It feels as if wrestling with the question is almost to doubt God's omnipotence or His provision for His people. Yet nothing is inappropriate about seeking a realistic understanding of the ministry environment and resource base provided to us by God. So we ask the question: What kind of financial resources are available to the Church in the United States today?

Is the Church Strapped for Cash?

One thing we may observe about our culture is that Americans are a money-conscious people. For millions of Americans, the chief money-related issue is their belief that they do not have enough money. Many people commit extraordinary amounts of mental, emotional and physical energy to worrying about money, protecting their money and seeking to acquire more money. For millions of other Americans, although they indisputably have enough money to live a comfortable and secure lifestyle, they believe their lives would be more satisfying if they simply had more discretionary funds. They, too, spend countless hours mulling about the possibilities of becoming wealthier.

For a privileged minority, their financial strain relates to having more resources than most people and not knowing how to handle their good fortune in ways that are personally, socially and morally responsible and fulfilling. Money, it seems, is often on our minds. More often than not, the nagging question with which we wrestle is how we can increase our wealth.

Organizations that have accepted the responsibility for helping people—including both churches and other charitable entities—ruminate about the same dilemma. The plague of insufficient funds is every bit as disturbing in the minds of church leaders as it is in the minds of those running nonreligious nonprofit organizations (NPOs). Yet the financial woes of Christian churches in the United States is not one that will bring tears of sorrow to the eyes of Christians outside the United States.

> **"IN REVELATIONS WE READ OF A BOOK WHICH NO MAN COULD OPEN. SOME BELIEVE THAT WAS THE POCKETBOOK." ANONYMOUS**

Christian congregations in the United States are, on average, the richest churches in the world. They possess buildings, land, vehicles, full-time salaried staff and technology ranging from telephones and flannel boards (low tech) to interactive satellite-delivered video conferences, and big-screen video projection that includes state-of-the-art computer-generated graphics and Internet web sites (high tech).

In spite of their privileged positions, our research shows that tens of thousands of pastors, who are well educated in biblical perspectives and cross-cultural dynamics, harbor serious concerns about not having sufficient funds to do the work they feel called to pursue. Besides the casual questions and comments I encounter from pastors, many church leaders regularly ask themselves, God and others this question: What could happen if God's people would release God's money to do God's work? How often have pastors lamented that part of their task is to raise enough money to do the work of the ministry—a responsibility that many, if not most, pastors ruefully accept as one of the less appealing parts of their jobs.

Are the ministries in the United States, particularly churches, financially crippled? Are many churches on the precipice of facing extinction because of a lack of funds? The answers to such questions depend on how you interpret information about the marketplace. The following raw data is useful for gaining a realistic perspective about the state of generosity and stewardship within the United States and the Church today.

- In the United States this year, individuals will donate more than $125 billion to all nonprofit organizations.[2]
- Of the money donated to all NPOs in 1996, a majority of the dollars came from born-again Christians. Although they represent only 38 percent of the adult population, the per capita giving of believers is several times that of nonbelievers, enabling them to

claim credit for most of the money donated to all religious, social and charitable activity.[3]

- More than $60 billion a year is donated to religious nonprofit organizations. The vast bulk of that sum—more than $40 billion annually—goes directly to churches, and almost all of it comes from individuals (that is, not from corporations or foundations).[4]
- In a typical month, 6 out of every 10 adults donate money to a church or other kind of nonprofit organization; three-fourths of all adults do so during the typical year.[5]
- During the course of a year, two out of every three adults who donate money to nonprofit organizations give some money to a church.[6]
- Among adults who attend church regularly (an average of at least once a month), more than one out of every three (37 percent) did not give any money to a church in the past year![7]
- In a typical year, 26 percent of adults who give money to a church also donated funds to religious nonprofits other than a church.[8]
- Overall, only 3 to 5 percent of the people who donate money to a church "tithe" their income—that is, give 10 percent or more of their money to religious organizations.[9]
- In spite of the fact that churches receive most of the funds donated to nonprofit organizations, the average annual church budget is less than $100,000.[10]
- The average donation by adults who attend Protestant churches is about $17 a week.[11]
- Among the 10 largest denominations in the United States, those whose churches receive support from the highest percentage of adherents are Presbyterian, Assemblies of God and Churches of Christ. The denominational churches that had the lowest proportions of attenders donating to the church were Episcopal, Pentecostal and Baptist.[12]
- Two out of three senior pastors of Protestant churches believe that their churches are not living up to their giving potential.[13]

Granted, there is constant discussion about whether or not people are giving what they should be giving to churches, as well as to other organizations that benefit society. No matter how you slice it, though, Americans are relatively generous donors of their money: No other nation in the world generates as much voluntary revenue for good works. On a per capita basis, the only nation that competes with the generosity of Americans is our northern neighbor, Canada.

The generosity of Americans, and their sensitivity to the needs of a wide range of people in the United States and throughout the world, helps to explain the existence of the more than 1.1 million tax-exempt, nonprofit organizations. Of that total, about 380,000 of them are churches and religious centers, including roughly 310,000 Protestant churches and about 20,000 Catholic churches. Although we already have more than 1 million organizations the government sanctions for tax-deductible giving, new nonprofit organizations are born every year. This proliferation of nonprofit entities would not persist if it were not for the charitable impulses of Americans and their willingness to work through these intermediaries to share their wealth with people and families in need.

We cannot deny the fact that Americans give a lot of money to their favorite religious causes. The $60 billion given to religious organizations towers over the amount given to the second most popular category of non-profit activity—education—by more than a three-to-one margin.[14]

Two Sides to the Coin

Although it is possible to paint a rosy picture related to fund-raising in the church context, I would do you a disservice if I did not acknowledge another dimension to this reality. As our culture continues to experience dramatic change, significant transformations are affecting every corner of ministry—even the financial practices and foundations of the Church. Although all the encouraging news I reported is true, so are the following challenging conditions.

- Giving to religious causes, in general, is declining.
- Giving to churches, overall, is declining.
- The average annual amount of money donated to churches, per person, is declining.
- The ways in which the new generations of donors—busters and boomers—give money is different from the ways in which the older generations—builders and seniors—give.
- Growing numbers of churches and parachurch ministries in the United States are competing for the limited pool of contributions.
- A strong perception remains that churches do not need money as much as other charities do.
- Fewer people give habitually. More and more donors, coming now from the boomer and buster generations, evaluate every gift they give very carefully. Compared to giving patterns two or three decades ago, people are less likely to donate money to any organization automatically.

- The kinds of religious activities that stimulate people to give are changing, just as their giving priorities outside the religious realm are in transition.

Many fund-raisers had considered church donations a given, as if they could reasonably assume that the Church is insulated from pernicious cultural trends and changes in giving attitudes. Such has proven not to be the case. Although the total amount of money being donated by Americans to charity continues to climb each year, religious organizations are receiving a shrinking share of a growing pie. Understanding what causes such shifts in altruistic behavior is important for churches in their struggle to remain effective agents of transformation in an increasingly gospel-resistant nation.

Fund-Raising or Stewardship?

As we move down the path of understanding money and ministry, some subtleties must be considered as we discuss the means of acquiring money to do institutional ministry. Perhaps the most significant distinction is that between fund-raising and stewardship. Neither of these terms is especially popular among the masses—and for good reason.

"Fund-raising" connotes slick appeals, hokey events, endless pulpit announcements and pleas, bake sales and car washes, and so on. The perception that churches care more about raising money than they care about enhancing people's lives has led many individuals to abandon or avoid churches.

> **"STEWARDSHIP IS AN EXPRESSION OF THE FRUIT OF CHRIST'S LIFE, THROUGH THE HOLY SPIRIT, IN US." ANONYMOUS**

Speaking about "stewardship," though, is not an acceptable alternative to many people either. Many who are familiar with the term consider it to be nothing more than a dressed-up, churchified synonym for fund-raising. As one elderly gentleman informed me after a seminar, "Son, some people call theft, 'wealth redistribution.' Some call swearing, 'honest communication.' Well, you can call this stuff 'stewardship,' but it's nothing more than fund-raising."

Unfortunately, if it has any connotation at all, to most Christians stewardship means nothing more than fund-raising. It encompasses much more, though. Stewardship refers to the practice of holding something in trust for someone else, a process of serving others by managing their assets in their absence. Peter Block describes stewardship as "accountability without control or compliance."[15]

Fund-raising may involve raising money, but that is only one part of the endeavor. Those who wish to raise money engage in procedures designed to elicit dollars from donors, seeking to meet a dollar goal. Stewardship may involve raising money, but the true challenge encompasses deploying a holistic approach to thinking about, acquiring, managing, righteously exploiting and enjoying the resources in question. The difference between fund-raising and stewardship is that between following the letter of the Law and the spirit of the Law.

The ideal is to raise funds as part of a larger focus on stewardship—the appropriate interaction with all the resources entrusted to you by God. Thus, stewardship operates in the spiritual realm, not simply in the world of finance. Although fund-raisers are evaluated on their ability to reach monetary goals, stewards are measured according to the quality of their lives in relation to the resources in their care. Fund-raisers have a laudable goal: to collect money so that activities that better society may take place. Stewards have the ultimate goal: to be obedient and pleasing to God. To the fund-raiser, the purpose of the activity is to enable or facilitate activity. The steward, in contrast, engages in stewardship behavior as an act of worship to God.

> **THE DIFFERENCE BETWEEN FUND-RAISING AND STEWARDSHIP IS THAT BETWEEN FOLLOWING THE LETTER OF THE LAW AND THE SPIRIT OF THE LAW.**

Assuming there is a common ground between those promoting stewardship and those engaged in fund-raising—let's define that common ground as securing sufficient funds to finance the ministry for the coming year—how does a fund-raiser differ in day-to-day activity from a promoter of stewardship? The fund-raiser uses techniques to persuade people to donate their money to a worthy cause or institution, to satisfy the operational goals and the organizational mission, accepting all donor motivations as equally valid, as long as they result in giving. The stewardship champion, on the other hand, seeks to mobilize people to optimize the effect of the resources they manage for God, to achieve God's ultimate purpose, as a means of serving God and His people.

Fund-Raising Versus Stewardship
Different Approaches to Resource Development

	FUND-RAISING	STEWARDSHIP
Purpose	Fund the desired activity	Worship God
Goal	Meet budget; pay the bills	Serve God with full integrity
Realm of activity	Financial	Spiritual
Source of resources	Donors	God
Guiding document	Institutional budget	Bible
Motivation to give	Satisfy personal needs/ emotions	Thank God; fulfill spiritual responsibility
Personal return on investment	Self-satisfaction; tax deduction	Joy of giving; blessing of obedience to God
Precipitating relationship	Cause, institution or individual	God
Primary outcome of a donation	A better society	Bonding with God; His trust justified
Reasons for not donating	Skepticism; caution; prefer other opportunities	Ignorance of responsibility; lack of commitment to God; confusion about responsibility

Whether you choose to pursue a fund-raising approach or a steward-ship approach, a key outcome of either approach is to secure sufficient funding to facilitate effective ministry.

What Are the Issues?

If the data suggest, then, that a substantial base of funds is available for ministry through churches, what are the real issues facing the American

Church as it strives to capitalize on the current interest in spirituality?

The rest of this book is devoted to addressing key issues confronting the Church in its quest to raise enough money to do great ministry. My research has uncovered the following points.

1. *Who gives money to the Church?* If we can better understand who gives money, we can develop fund-raising efforts that are responsive to the unique needs, interests, characteristics, insights and expectations of those donors. We do not want to compromise what the Church stands for, but we do need to contextualize fund development strategies.

2. *Why do people give?* By discerning the motivations of church donors, we can better educate them so they may embrace more appropriate motives, as well as build church-based opportunities and responses around those ministries that excite the congregation.

3. *What do church people not understand about stewardship?* One of the Church's duties is to equip people to be better servants of God. A major barrier to godly service is ignorance of God's principles. Once we identify the barriers to a biblical understanding of money, sharing, donating and investing, we can help people possess a biblically accurate understanding of the issues and opportunities.

4. *How do churches effectively and efficiently raise money these days?* Our study of the churches that have most effectively raised donations for ministry sheds light on how basic biblical principles can be applied in today's content for tomorrow's ministry applications. Good stewardship mandates that we take both efficiency and effectiveness seriously. What does that look like at the end of the twentieth century?

5. *What is the role of church leaders in fund-raising and financial management in the church?* We know that most people respond to effective leadership, but what does effective leadership in the realm of church stewardship mean?

In the forthcoming chapters, we will answer these questions in ways that should give a pastor, a church staff person or a lay leader practical handles about how to conceive, plan, implement and evaluate fund-raising efforts in a church. Every church will apply the ideas and principles identified differently to account for the church's unique context. The principles described, however, are readily transferable to most situations. It is the task of the leader to understand the church's context, the stewardship conditions and principles and to devise a strategy to efficiently and comprehensively employ these principles.

Make no mistake about it, though. Billions and billions of dollars are already being given to the work of churches. More is readily available if we understand the environment and our people. How badly do you want to raise more money for your church?

Notes

1. This is not his real name.
2. *Giving USA 1996* (New York: AAFRC Trust for Philanthropy, 1996).
3. The data on which this is based come from a trio of nationwide surveys conducted by Barna Research Group, Ltd. among adults from July 1995 through July 1996. Those surveys involved interviews about giving behavior by talking to more than 3,000 adults randomly selected from the 48 contiguous states. Throughout this book when the expression "born-again Christian" is used, I am referring to people who are categorized by Barna Research as such, based upon their answers to two survey questions. The first question asks adults if they have ever made a personal commitment to Jesus Christ that is still important in their lives today. Among the people who reply in the affirmative, we pose a second question regarding life after death on earth. The person hears seven possible post-death experiences and is asked to choose the one that comes closest to describing what he or she believes will happen after death. The selection that classifies the person as a born-again Christian is: "When I die I will go to heaven because I have confessed my sins and accepted Jesus Christ as my Savior." We do not ask people to classify themselves as born again because our testing has shown that many who categorize themselves as born-again Christians also acknowledge they do not have any kind of ongoing, personal relationship with Christ, and many self-described born-again Christians are relying primarily upon their best efforts to earn a place in heaven or eternal salvation.
4. *Giving USA 1996* (New York: AAFRC Trust for Philanthropy, 1996).
5. Based on data from OmniPoll™ 1-96, January 1996, N=1004; and OmniPoll™ 2-96, July 1996, N=1006. Both surveys were conducted by the Barna Research Group, Ltd.
6. Based on data from OmniPoll™ 1-96, January 1996, N=1004; and OmniPoll™ 2-96, July 1996, N=1006. Both surveys were conducted by the Barna Research Group, Ltd.
7. Based on data from OmniPoll™ 1-96, January 1996, N=1004, conducted by the Barna Research Group, Ltd.
8. Based on data from OmniPoll™ 1-96, January 1996, N=1004, conducted by the Barna Research Group, Ltd.
9. Based on data from OmniPoll™ 2-96, July 1996, N=1006, conducted by the Barna Research Group, Ltd.
10. Based on PastorPoll™ 1-94, April 1994, N=402, conducted by the Barna Research Group, Ltd.
11. Based on data from OmniPoll™ 1-96, January 1996, N=1004; and OmniPoll™ 2-96, July 1996, N=1006, both conducted by the Barna Research Group, Ltd.
12. Data from the *Yearbook of American and Canadian Churches*, Kenneth Bedell, ed. (Nashville: Abingdon Press, 1996).
13. Based on PastorPoll™ 1-94, April 1994, N=402, conducted by the Barna Research Group, Ltd.
14. *Giving USA 1996* (New York: AAFRC Trust for Philanthropy, 1996).
15. Peter Block, *Stewardship* (San Francisco: Berrett Koehler Publishers, 1993), p. xx.

2

Myths, Legends and Assumptions About Church Donors

"HE IS NO FOOL WHO GIVES UP WHAT HE CANNOT
KEEP IN ORDER TO GAIN WHAT HE CANNOT LOSE."
JIM ELLIOT

One of the most deceptive and insidious barriers to advancing good stewardship within churches is the vast array of assumptions we possess and act upon regarding money, ministry and donors. Those assumptions might be thought of as myths: notions we revere, or alleged "facts" we take for granted, but which are falsehoods. Drawing from the research we conducted among both church leaders and the donors themselves, let's confront a few of the most popular myths and set the record straight. Chances are, once you begin to think more critically about the assumptions you hold regarding money, ministry and donors, you will begin to identify even more of these stewardship deceptions that have held you in their power.

Boomers Don't Give

Myth: Given their achievement orientation and their selfish nature, boomers generally do not donate much money to churches or other charities.

Truth: Boomers are the most generous givers the nation has seen this century. They may no longer wear bell-bottoms, listen to psychedelic rock or engage in love-ins, but they have retained their desire to influence the world, and one of the ways they do so is through their investment of time and money.

Some have contested the idea that boomers are generous. Their giving has to be understood in context. If we compare their giving to that of prior generations when those people were the same age, boomers emerge as more generous. Their level of giving is sometimes questioned because boomers are also the richest generation we have ever had, so observers have high expectations of them. The people who are questioning their level of generosity tend to be older, have also amassed significant wealth (and have reduced family obligations) and expect others to be as proportionally generous as they are.

Another reason boomers are chastised is because they do not give as large a proportion of their aggregate contributions to churches as have prior generations. Placed in context, however, the problem is not that they are not willing to give to churches, but that they have not been given a sufficient motivation to do so. Boomers, by our culture's standards, are generous givers, but they give their money away based on different criteria than did prior generations. This sometimes makes them perplexing or frustrating to older church leaders who do not understand what drives boomers, and thus are unsuccessful at raising money from them.

Myth: People who are conservative theologically, ideologically and philosophically do not give money to ministry ventures associated with liberalism. Similarly, those who are mostly liberal in their vantage point and lifestyle do not donate funds to conservative ministry programs.

Truth: One of our recent research studies uncovered some mind-boggling giving patterns. A large proportion of people who give to conservative parachurch ministries also give to liberal parachurch organizations—even though the organizations promote opposite sides of the same issue—or approach those issues from entirely different directions. For instance, a substantial number of households donate to both Focus on the Family, the conservative, pro-life ministry, and Planned Parenthood, the liberal, pro-abortion organization.

We often assume that when people give money to a church or to a parachurch ministry they do so after serious reflection and have ideologically consistent, theologically defensible, well-conceived convictions. The truth is that millions of church donors give money for a complex web of reasons that may seem, in some ways, contradictory. The study showed us that what church leaders perceive to be the primary purpose or "selling point" of their ministry or program may have little or nothing to do with a particular donor's motivations for supporting such ministry activity.

Myth: Driven by their concern about the spiritual needs and development of their own children, parents who have kids under the age of 18 living in their home are more likely than are empty nesters to fund missionaries, evangelistic activities or work geared toward providing international relief and development.
Truth: Parents who have children living in their households are more attracted to localized giving opportunities. They are the most prolific donors to youth work, but also to other kinds of endeavors designed to enhance the quality of life in their geographic area.

Myth: As stewards of God's creation, Christians are more likely than nonbelievers to respond positively to ministries, programs and campaigns built around environmental and wildlife protection.
Truth: Believe it or not, Christians are substantially less likely than are non-Christians to fund efforts designed to protect the environment or animal life. Most believers do not think of themselves as stewards of God's money, much less stewards of other aspects of His creation. Even attitudinally, Christians are no more interested in environmental protection than are nonbelievers.

Myth: The higher the household's income, the more likely they are to donate money every month.
Truth: Actually, we discovered that people from middle- and lower-income households are slightly more likely to give on a monthly basis to organizations, such as churches, than are the wealthiest among us. There is, of course, a necessary distinction between the size of gifts and the frequency of those gifts. People from upper-income households are more likely to give fewer donations, but to give larger amounts, than are those of lesser means. People from wealthier households also give to fewer organizations, while people from middle- or lower-income households prefer to spread their limited money to benefit many organizations.

Myth: Most donors believe a relationship with an organization they support, including their primary church, is absolutely necessary for them to continue to give funds.

Truth: Only about 4 out of every 10 donors think this way. To a majority of people who give to churches, such a relationship is deemed a bonus, and may solidify their financial commitment to the church. Most people, however, are willing to give to a church they regularly attend without thinking they need a true relationship with the organization. (For more discussion about what a "relationship" with a nonprofit organization means, see chapter 4.)

We also learned that most people who donate to churches do not feel a driving need to have some kind of relationship with those who benefit directly from their donations. A willingness remains to give anonymously, as long as the donor is cognizant of results achieved through giving.

Myth: When donors encounter a well-documented and carefully conceived budget, they are compelled to fund the plan.

Truth: Donors give to people. They have no interest in institutions, documents or campaigns, per se. Well-crafted, persuasive plans that include accompanying budgets may provide a level of psychological comfort to donors. The mere presence of plans, briefs, schedules, budgets and other documents, however, fails to stimulate the interest of most church donors. They assume such documents exist. If they determine that the planning that facilitates stewardship documentation has not occurred, they may balk at giving. Such documentation is a necessary but insufficient factor to prompt most people to donate to a church.

Myth: Donors already feel bombarded by information; the last thing they want is access to more facts and figures regarding how the church uses their money.

Truth: Because we are a skeptical society, a well-educated nation and we want to protect our money as well as possible, donors appreciate access to information regarding how their contributions are used and what effect their giving has had. It is true that donors are overwhelmed by information in the normal course of their daily activities. They receive security, however, from knowing that documentation of how their donations were used is readily available.

In our work with parachurch ministries, for instance, we have discovered that more than four out of five donors say they will not donate to a ministry that does not make financial statements available to donors. At the same time, we also know that fewer than 1 out of every 10 donors to ministries ever requests a financial statement from the ministries supported. In several situations, we found that a majority of donors who receive financial statements give them a cursory read, at best, before devoting the bulk of their attention to narrative descriptions of the ministry.

Myth: Donors would rather just give their donations and stay at arm's length from the decision makers of the ministry than provide advice, ideas and other input to the leaders of the church.
Truth: Donors may not want to know the people their money will help, but they often love to provide their views about how such ministry should be conducted. For some, this is a means of protecting their investment. For others, gaining decision-making input is one of the tangible benefits of their giving. Most church donors, though, appreciate opportunities to add their thoughts as one means of "owning" the ministry in which they are investing. For donors who are 50 or older, in particular, their advice usually comes without strings attached.

Myth: As long as a fund-raising event includes a free meal, donors are excited about attending.
Truth: There is more than a little truth to the notion that Christians like to attend events that include a meal. (Realize, incidentally, that the days of the potluck meal are generally past. Most church people do not cook meals for themselves these days; the prospects of cooking food for people they do not know are getting slimmer and slimmer each year.) Our research noted, however, that when people attend a fund-raiser these days, they want a full entertainment experience. It is not enough to eat a mediocre meal and listen to an average after-dinner speaker. If they are carving precious time out of their packed schedules, they want an enjoyable, professional experience. A meal may be part of that experience, but donors these days have higher expectations.

As you can see, understanding the minds and hearts of donors is a complicated task. Many of the assumptions that used to be true are true no more. Do you possess other assumptions about who gives money, why they give and how to strategically raise revenue? Do any of these assumptions need to be reexamined in view of the changing attitudes, values, experiences and needs of the people who support your church?

Credibility Is Critical

One of the most encouraging conclusions we may reach from the research is that in spite of the scandals reported in recent years, American donors have a high level of confidence in the financial credibility of religious centers and churches. Nearly half the donors we interviewed (47 percent) think the money they donate to churches and places of worship is used more productively than is the money they give to other kinds of nonprofit organizations. Another 4 in 10 (38 percent) think the money they donate to places of worship is used with equal effectiveness to that which is given to other organizations. Only 3 percent of adults indicated greater confidence in nonprofit organizations than in churches when it comes to the efficient use of donated funds.

Appealing to Ideology

A crucial insight that emerged from the research is that Americans are not ideological in their giving. Although many sermons, church programs and stewardship campaigns are founded on the notion of an "us versus them" battle built along ideological lines, the research underscored that most adults are uncomfortable with black-and-white dichotomies of reality. Rather than perceive the world in such confrontational ways, they tend to see everything as related to everything else, which, therefore, requires sensitivity and a softer edge in communications and activity.

Granted, millions of people have a clear and central sense of ideology that compels them to give—and to give big time. The majority of church attenders, however, are not seeking a ministry that is looking for an enemy, but one that is offering a kinder, gentler world—a place of security and respite. Campaigns based on a fear-of-the-enemy or fight-to-win mentality rather than a love-your-neighbor mentality will excite some, but repulse most.

Many people who are sensitive to ideological distinctions are usually not driven by a true philosophy of life or worldview that limits their charitable options. Those who are generally conservative in social, political and theological matters may in fact donate to a conservative ministry. They are not giving because of the extended conservative agenda advanced by the organization, however, but because they personally hold a conservative position on one or two concepts about which the ministry maintains the same position (e.g., conservative positions about abortion or homosexuality). More often than not, people give to a church affiliated with a particular denomination not because of the denomination's doctrine and policy positions, but because of what that church is doing in the community and in the donor's life.

Planned Giving

Most donors have a will or estate plan. More than 9 out of 10 of those donors, however, have not included a church as one of the recipients of a portion of their estates. A viable way of upgrading aggregate revenues to a nonprofit organization (NPO) is to develop credibility, relationships and willingness to incorporate the NPO as a beneficiary. As the congregational mass in America ages, and as the aging church attenders show less inclination to leave their entire estates to family, those organizations that demonstrate a realistic interest in becoming a beneficiary will have an advantage.

How can a church attract legacies? It will take an intentional effort not only to inform people of the possibility of supporting the church through their estate plans, but also to offer assistance in including the church within their documents. Because this is primarily an activity of interest and relevance to older adults, such a campaign could easily be targeted to the senior members of the congregation. Realize that such a campaign need not be considered a nuisance or potential irritant. Other research we have conducted has shown that increasing numbers of seniors are actively searching for worthy causes to which they can leave a chunk of their assets. Many seniors have decided they should give at least some of their assets to causes (in many cases, all of their assets) and not just to their families.

Developing Relationships

From the very start, the Church was intended to be a *community* of believers, sharing relationships with each other as well as with Jesus Christ. In that context, it is alluring to conceive of fund-raising as a relational activity in which the donor gives out of a sense of loyalty and devotion to the church—that is, out of a sense of being bonded to the faith community. Although the notion of establishing a relationship with donors is conceptually arresting, our interviews with donors indicate that most of them are neither overtly searching for such a connection, nor are they expecting one to develop. This probably says more about their expectations regarding church ministry than about fund-raising realities.

We cannot afford to ignore the fact, though, that a church typically exerts its most significant influence when meaningful relationships exist among the people. These relationships should allow ministry principles and truths to penetrate the protective shell each of us builds to become insulated from criticism or change. Relationships are a natural pursuit for a church. Those relationships may not enhance financial support, but they ought to be pursued as a means of facilitating the family of believers as Christ intended.

Not surprisingly, the concept of having a relationship with a church, or with any nonprofit entity for that matter, varies significantly among donors. For some it implies knowing other donors; to many it relates to acts of personal service to or through the entity. To others it insinuates having been helped by the NPO; to some it simply relates to being aware of the activities of the organization. To yet another segment, it relates to being united with the group through common beliefs, a mutual sense of commitment to a cause. As in interpersonal relationships, then, expectations and abilities span the spectrum when it comes to donor-recipient relationships.

One danger we should avoid is that of developing effective procedures and systems that become mechanical. Such programs often become emotionally sterile and rob a church of the joys of seeing God change us through the stewardship process.

Some professional fund-raisers have posited that donors are not so much interested in a relationship as they are in receiving respect from the organizations they support. In our view, this is slicing the data too thin and creating a false dichotomy. Our read of the marketplace is that the vast majority of donors expect their churches to treat them with genuine respect. They would like to have a relationship, although it is probably not necessary for continued financial support, as long as the other persuasive factors are in place (e.g., the cause, efficiency, efficacy, trust, benefits).

The High Touch Society

A decade ago, John Naisbitt spoke of the coming of a "high tech, high touch" culture. His prediction has come true. We now live in a world that is being reshaped and redefined every day by sophisticated technology. One of the outgrowths of the technological encroachment is that people need to have a sense of human connection in the midst of a software-driven world.

In the local church, this is translated in the hearts of donors knowing they count as individuals, not just as faceless sources of money facilitating the conduct of worthwhile ministry activity. Most church donors desire accessibility to the thrones of power within the church—starting with, but not limited to, the senior pastor. Having the ability to converse with key decision makers and ministry leaders—whether in person, by electronic means or through secondary means—is a major plus in the eyes of the donor. We have seen that the churches that emphasize accessibility and two-way communication raise more money—and they raise it more easily—than do churches in which the fund-raising procedures are hierarchical and formal.

Money Through Events

Event marketing was big in the late 1980s and early 1990s. It appears this form of fund-raising may have run its course. People's interest in small-scale events is very limited. Major events may have somewhat greater appeal, but even that varies largely by the donor segment in question. When it comes to the kind of localized, comparatively small-scale events churches often sponsor, the event is likely to be seen as providing hollow personal benefits or, worse, as little more than a means of manipulation or a nuisance.

The prognosis for events is not upbeat. Events conflict with people's desire to protect their time. The feeling of those in the church who are responsible for developing the event is that their efforts generally result in disappointing financial results. Our surveys of congregations typically find that the people in the pews dread an upcoming all-church event. They feel pressure to attend (and, perhaps, to donate) even when they do not feel good about the event, or the ministry or program that it benefits. Events usually raise comparatively minimal amounts of money. Only the heartiest of church leaders would rely even moderately upon events as a substantial source of future funding.

Build for the Future

Many churches invest in the present, alone. Instead of recognizing that financial commitment takes a lifetime to shape and develop, the emphasis is placed solely upon those people who will provide an immediate positive return for the church. Young adults inevitably get left behind. Unfortunately, many of them never catch on or catch up to stewardship realities.

Young adults need to cultivate the practice of biblical stewardship. In the early stages of the process, churches may not receive much in return in the way of dollars or in frequency of gifts. Young people may not be as loyal to the ministry as we would like. The practice of stewardship, though, is one that takes time and training to unfold. Ministries that fail to invest resources in the developmental process today will reap the negative rewards of shortsightedness in the future.

Send Reinforcements

It is tempting to assume that once someone gives money to a church the person emotionally "owns" the ministry. That, unfortunately, is a dangerous assumption. It is vitally important to reinforce people's decisions. Many donors to churches give their money without full knowledge of what their generosity will accomplish, or how important the act of giving is to them and to the church. Most donors receive solicitations for funds from other worthwhile causes, and in spite of their decision to support the church, they may continue to wrestle with questions of appropriateness and efficacy. All donors have the same human need to be encouraged in their desires to be agents of spiritual transformation in a culture that disparages such commitments. Reinforcing the act of giving works for a variety of reasons at various emotional and intellectual levels.

One effective means of reinforcement is to continually promote the church as a person's first and primary channel of influence in a hurting world. Remind people of the spiritual benefits they receive from the church. Tell the story of how the church has benefited other people through its outreach ministries. Extend sincere gratitude for the role the donor has played in making effective ministry possible. In short, pay attention to people's ongoing need to feel good about their choices.

3

Who Are the Donors to Churches?

"THOSE WHO GIVE HAVE ALL THINGS.

THOSE WHO WITHHOLD HAVE NOTHING."

HINDU PROVERB

To understand who church donors are, we can evaluate them on three unique dimensions: their personal backgrounds (demographics); their attitudes and values (psychographics); and their spiritual perspectives and practices (theolographics™). Viewing church donors through this three-stage filter offers a holistic perception of the people who provide resources for church-based ministry.

The personal attributes of donors (i.e., demographic characteristics) are the elements about donors that are most commonly examined. I have spent a decade exploring demographics and donor behavior for a wide array of ministries and other charitable organizations, including many churches and parachurch ministries. From this research I know that demographics are only moderately useful in predicting whether or not a person is likely to donate to charitable activity or to a church, how often they will donate and the level of their generosity. Having noted the limitations of demographic analysis, though, let me indicate that people who donate to churches have a somewhat different profile from those who do not contribute to the financial well-being of a church. The following information is a rundown of the demographic nature of church donors, in comparison to non-supporters.[1]

Demographics of Church Donors

Thank God for Busters and Builders

Church donors tend to be older than nongivers (44 years old, compared to 37 among adults who do not support a church). This is not unexpected because we also know that the adults who regularly attend church services and those who actively participate in church life also tend to be older than the norm.

Marked giving patterns are discernible according to generational lines.[2] Baby busters, who currently range in age from the mid-teens to the early thirties, are the least likely to give. Among the adult portion of that group, just 30 percent have donated any money to a church in the past year. Baby boomers are considerably more generous—45 percent of those in their mid-thirties to early fifties have donated to a church. The builder generation, which is currently in the early fifties to late sixties age bracket, is clearly the most generous of the four adult generations. Of the builders in their fifties, nearly 6 out of every 10 have donated to a church in the past year (58 percent). That level dips to 50 percent among builders who are in their sixties, likely due to the financial difficulties experienced by many retired and ailing people. Among adults in their seventies and beyond, referred to herein as the seniors generation, more than half (52 percent) have given to a church in the prior 12 months.

To fully understand how age correlates with church giving, we must also consider church attendance. Not surprisingly, the younger the adult, the less likely the person is to attend church services and, consequently, to donate money. Conversely, the older the adult, the more common it is for the person to attend church services regularly and—until reaching age 60— to give money to the church regularly and generously. The pattern clearly changes around the age of 60. At that point, church attendance remains above the norm, but the proportion of people giving actually declines (due to the radical economic shift that typically accompanies reaching the traditional age of retirement or employment deceleration).

One way of achieving a more precise understanding of giving proclivity by age is to assess giving among those who attend churches, rather than evaluating giving simply by generational ties. Social scientists refer to this statistical process as "holding a variable constant"—in this case, we would examine giving behavior while holding church attendance constant (i.e., study giving and attending jointly to better understand the correlation between them and a person's age). When we do so, a major surprise emerges. The age groups most likely to give are baby busters and builders. Finding this to be true for builders is no surprise, but how can we explain the altruistic behavior of the youngest adult segment?

This emerging generation is less likely than the norm to attend Protestant or Catholic church activities and less likely to include involvement in a

Christian church as part of its lifestyle. Busters who have made a commitment to a church, however, are unusually keen about the pursuit of their faith or about making a concerted effort to be a significant part of a community of faith. We also learn that among church goers, the age group least likely to support churches are older boomers (those in their mid-forties and early fifties) and retired adults (most frequently those 65 or older).

Don't Reject the Educated

The prevailing assumption is that the more educated people are, the less likely they are to attend church services and to commit their money to church work. Our data show that just the opposite is true regarding financial support. Half of all college-educated adults give money to a church during the course of a year. That compares to about 4 out of 10 who donate to churches among those who attended but did not graduate from college (44 percent of whom are church donors) or among church regulars who never attended college (42 percent).

Holding church attendance constant shows that the same pattern prevails: Among all who attend church, the more highly educated they are, the more likely they are to give. This may be related to the fact that higher levels of education are closely associated with higher income levels, a deeper sense of social and community responsibility and a greater feeling of influence through various means of personal involvement in social institutions. It is important to note, though, that educational achievement is not a major influencer of church giving. These data are perhaps most useful in encouraging us to dismiss the myth that well-educated people do not support churches.

Ask Mom and Dad for Money

According to the old saying, "If you want something to get done, assign it to the busiest person." When it comes to church finances, we might modify the axiom to read, "If you want to raise money, approach the people who have the highest expenses." In this case, we would seek money from families.

Married adults are significantly more likely to help fund a church than are single adults. In some ways this is not surprising because single adults are generally younger and have lower income levels. Married adults also typically represent two-income households, enabling those families to earn a greater sum of money, on average, than would be true for the typical single adult.

One of the fastest-growing segments of the single-adult population is that of single parents—which, in our culture, usually means a single mother and her children. Given that single parents often live on the edge of poverty, it is not surprising to discover that single adults are less likely to donate to churches, and that those who contribute provide smaller sums of money than do other adults of the same age.

The Ethnic Gap

Intriguingly, although religion plays a more central role in the lives of black adults, white adults are nearly 50 percent more likely than black adults to donate to a church during the course of a year. Our research has consistently indicated that African-Americans are more likely than are Caucasians to possess orthodox Christian views, to attend church services regularly and to describe religion as an important part of their lives. However, just one-third of all black adults donate to a church in a typical year, considerably less than is true among white adults (half of whom donate during the year). Among people from other ethnic groups, support for churches is even lower. Only one-quarter of all adults who are Hispanic, Asian, Native American or of some other ethnic origin donate money to a church.

When we hold church attendance constant, however, we discover that whites and non-Caucasians other than blacks are similar in their likelihood of giving to a church. The black population stands out as particularly unlikely to support their local church. This might be attributed to lower household income levels, lower levels of education and cultural distinctives within African-American churches and the black community.

Political Deception

The vast majority of people who donate to churches are registered voters. This, in itself, is not surprising because registered voters in America outnumber unregistered voters by a three to one margin. The conventional wisdom is that the higher likelihood of giving by registered voters is reflective of their greater interest in societal health and their heightened willingness or desire to share a degree of responsibility for the condition of the nation.

This widely accepted conclusion may seem logical, but it is probably not accurate. When we factor in church attendance the outcome changes. Among adults who are not registered voters, relatively few attend church: They are only half as likely to be in church next Sunday as are registered voters. Unregistered voters who do attend church, however, are substantially *more* likely than registered voters who attend church to donate funds to the church's work.

Many unregistered voters have chosen not to register because they do not believe the political process is a means to meaningful social change or personal benefit. Consequently, the unregistered voters who attend church harbor neither the illusion nor the hope that government will change or positively influence people's lives. Yet they do hold such hope for the church and are willing to give money to support that hope.

Diluting the Conservatives

Where people stand on the key social and political issues of the day is related to their church attendance and to their giving. We consistently find that those who have conservative views about matters of politics and public affairs are more likely to attend church services, and are more likely to attend such services frequently, than are people who hold middle-of-the-road or liberal viewpoints.

Once again, though, a closer evaluation of the facts, rather than reliance upon assumptions, uncovers some surprising truths. Despite the relentless attention the mass media focus upon the alleged deep pockets of the "religious right," our research shows that those who are ideologically centrist or liberal are more likely to give to the churches they attend than are those who have conservative views. Overall, 56 percent of all self-described conservatives have given to a church in the past year, compared to 45 percent of the middlers and 34 percent of the liberals. When the same figures are run only for those who attend church, however, we discover that the nonconservative contingent was 17 percent more likely to support church work financially.

The comparatively limited financial support provided to churches by those on the ideological right is largely attributable to the fact that conservatives are nearly twice as likely as moderates or liberals to donate funds to religious organizations other than churches (i.e., parachurch ministries). In addition, they are about 70 percent more likely to give money to political parties or advocacy groups than are nonconservatives. In other words, conservatives are more likely than others to give away greater amounts of money, in total, during the year; to donate to a broader spectrum of organizations; and to support entities in addition to their church to help achieve their goals.

In Defense of the Affluent

Naturally, we would expect wealthier people to be more likely to donate their money to worthy causes. The data support this expectation: The higher the household income of an individual, the more likely the person is to give money to a church. Whereas one-fourth of all households earn less than $20,000 annually, only one-fifth of those households donate to churches. At the other end of the income continuum, although one-third of all households earn $40,000 a year or more, those same households represent two-fifths of the donor homes.

> **"MAKE ALL YOU CAN, SAVE ALL YOU CAN, GIVE ALL YOU CAN." JOHN WESLEY**

When we remove adults who do not attend church from the equation, we find the pattern changes a bit. High-income households (i.e., those making $75,000 a year or more) remain the most likely to give money to a church. The next most likely group, though, are those in the $30,000 to $50,000 income bracket. The households sandwiched in between those two income segments (i.e., the $50,000 to $75,000 group) are considerably less likely to support a church financially. The households earning annual incomes under $30,000 are among the least likely to donate to a church.

Although evidence supports the contention that more affluent people give a smaller proportion of their yearly income to churches than do those who are less financially secure, the typical affluent person does give a greater absolute sum to churches than does the typical middle-class or lower-class person.

Don't Write Off Men

Women are consistently more active in the church than are men. They are more likely to attend services, volunteer, read the Bible regularly, pray daily, attend Sunday School classes, attend small-group meetings for spiritual growth and invite non-Christians to visit their church or church activities. The same pattern of personal investment is true when it comes to giving money to their church. Although 41 percent of all men have given financial support to a church in the past year, nearly half of all women (47 percent) have done so.

However, when we eliminate the influence of higher levels of church attendance among women (they are nearly 50 percent more likely than men to attend church on any given Sunday), we discover that when men do attend, they are *more* likely than women to donate money to the church.

Gold in the West

Significant differences are also noticeable geographically. As would be expected, the areas of the nation that have the smallest proportion of church donors are the West and the Northeast. In these large regions—which together encompass about half the nation's population—donors cumulatively represent barely one-quarter of the nation's church donors. The majority of donors come from the South, the Southwest and the Midwest.

Holding church attendance constant results in an entirely different portrait of reality. The areas in which people who attend church are most likely to give money to a church are the Mountain and Pacific Coast states—that is, the Western region. The area in which church attendance is very high but giving is weakest is the Southwest (Texas, New Mexico, Arizona, Oklahoma), and the South is not much different.

Church Attendance Changes Things

Demographically, then, we have learned that church attendance must be taken into account before drawing conclusions about giving patterns. Failing to do so often leads to erroneous assumptions about who is most likely to give money to a church. In summary, then, we know that among adults who attend church services, those most inclined to donate to churches are busters and builders, married adults (especially those who have school-age kids), people who are not registered to vote, those who do not have a conservative political ideology, men, whites and affluent people.

Remember, too, that although these segments reflect the people who might be most likely to give financial support to a church if they attend, these are not necessarily the segments that are most likely to attend. Consequently, these high-proclivity segments may not represent the greatest number of people located within the pews; rather, they constitute those who are most likely to donate if you can get them into the pews.

Invading the Mind and the Heart

If demographics define the socioeconomic history of an individual or group, psychographics tell us about what is happening inside these people. Psychographics explore the attitudes, the values and life perspectives of a person. Fund-raisers have long believed that if you comprehend what is important to potential donors and understand how they perceive reality, then you have a better chance of influencing their thoughts and behaviors through your communication and outreach efforts.

In a prior study, I discovered that as fascinating and seductive as psychographic analysis may be, these measures are poor predictors of whether or not a person becomes a donor to a charitable, nonprofit organization.[3] Is the same lack of value true for psychographics in relation to giving to churches?

Self-Perceptions
Church donors generally describe themselves differently than do people who do not support churches financially, but only in terms of their personal religious perspectives. When it comes to nonreligious adjectives, donors and nondonors are equally likely to describe themselves as happy, excited about life, too busy, stressed out, superstitious, wealthy and lonely. The distinctions that arise are related to religious descriptions. For instance, church donors are more likely than nondonors to say they are religious or to describe themselves as "born-again Christians."

Life Outcomes
Amazingly, the lifestyle conditions and life outcomes deemed very desirable by both church donors and those who do not donate to a church are nearly identical. In the rare instances of points of divergence, those dissimilarities usually relate to religious perspectives and goals. Church donors

are much more likely to cite a close relationship with God, being part of a local church and having an influence on other people's lives as being very desirable.

Other conditions for which there are discernible differences include the desire to have close, personal friendships and to have a clear purpose for living—both are characteristics church donors are more likely to consider very desirable than are nondonors. Regarding the more mundane aspects of lifestyle and world perspective—as measured by the other eight items in our research—there were no distinctions between donors and nondonors.

Although there may not be many differences, the distinctions that emerge are enlightening. Once again, the lesson is that a substantial proportion of church donors are driven to achieve or experience a deeper spiritual life, as manifested by the depth of their relationship with God, the sense of community with fellow believers and the ability to influence the lives of others. These are classic outcomes of a meaningful Christian faith. People who are able to experience such outcomes, especially through the enablement provided by their church, are more likely to support the work of their church. It is, after all, not only biblically appropriate, but also personally beneficial.

As you might expect, the people who attend churches but do not donate to them are usually driven by the desire to achieve comfort and worldly success more than by a desire to know, serve and please God. Church, to these noncontributors, is not a family of faith of which they are an integral part as much as it is a means to a tangible, earthly end. Nongiving attenders have the highest level of desire for good health, a comfortable lifestyle, a high-paying job, owning a large home and achieving fame. They are lowest on the continuum in terms of the importance of friendships.

We have also discovered that donors and nondonors are nearly identical in the importance they assign to a wide array of life possibilities. When asked to assess the importance of 11 items, there was no difference in the relative importance assigned to money, time, friendships, family, career, personal health, politics and government. There was evidence of a difference of opinion in relation to just three items: the importance of religion, the Bible and their community. Once again, the primary points of disparity between church donors and nondonors are related to religious or spiritual realities.

Change

Change is one of the most controversial, misunderstood and relentless forces in modern life. People's circumstances and environment change continually and significantly. Personal, cultural and situational changes—even those transformations that are healthy or desirable—produce stress. Substantial levels of change—either many small changes occurring simultaneously, or one or more major, cataclysmic changes occurring in a person's life—can initiate a comprehensive restructuring of a person's perceptions, obligations and relationships.

At the very least, significant changes in a person's life produce a new balance among preexisting relationships and responsibilities. During times of significant change, many people who had been ardent supporters of a church discontinue their financial support (as well as their participation in church activities and ministries). Because our lives are a complex, multidimensional blend of experiences and relationships, when one element changes, the entire mix changes.

Not surprisingly, then, we learned that people whose lives are relatively stable are more likely to donate to a church. Adults who experience relatively minimal change in their lives are considerably more likely to provide—and to continue to provide—financial support to a church.

Based on the seven indicators of lifestyle change we evaluated, we found that people who donate to churches are, on average, 36 percent more likely to have experienced stability in those dimensions of their lives than are the people whose lives are characterized by significant change.

For example, a change of residence is a major transition that may trigger a revision of church giving patterns. You can see this reality clearly in churches located in areas of high transience (e.g., military communities, college towns, central city). Those ministries are no less worthy of donations than are churches in less transient locations, yet they typically experience a comparatively difficult struggle to raise money for the continuing operation of the church and its ministry.

Attitudes and Values
The aspect of psychographics most frequently explored by researchers is that of people's attitudes and values. "Attitudes and values" cover a lot of territory. If we take an overview of people's attitudes and values and relate those perspectives to the proclivity of adults to contribute to a church, we discover some important truths about the ability to increase the church's revenue base.

One important component of people's attitudes and values concerns views about the nature of people and the significance of interpersonal relationships. The differences between donors and nondonors in these matters are slight. For instance, donors were only a bit less trusting of other people, but at the same time emerged as somewhat less concerned about the ability to make lasting friendships these days.

The most telling distinction, however, related to views about the family. Donors were clearly much more supportive of the traditional family, as four-fifths of them (78 percent) believe that if the traditional family falls apart, American society will collapse. In contrast, just three-fifths of all nondonors (61 percent) echoed the same feelings about the significance of the traditional family. It is noteworthy that a similar proportion of those who attend churches but do not donate concurred with this statement. Certainly, most people consider the family to be an important institution.

We found that if a church focuses substantial energy and attention on family solidarity and development, such emphasis is appreciated but will not increase most people's loyalty to, or investment in, that ministry: such an emphasis is expected. On the other hand, to the most committed church donors, the church's effort to strengthen the family is often deemed one of the most important ministries of the church.

Character

As millions of Americans search for meaning, purpose and values, the morality, ethics and personal values of donors is related to their giving patterns. Most Americans share a belief that America is in a moral crisis. Where the views of donors and nondonors differ the most relates to the specifics of how morality and values are practiced.

The lightning rods tend to be the high-profile, controversial issues such as homosexuality, abortion, the role of women in ministry and divorce. Church donors are considerably more likely than nondonors to take a conservative viewpoint (e.g., homosexual behavior or having an abortion is immoral).

This does not mean church donors always take the high road in their personal lives. Nearly two out of five donors (36 percent) contend that "sometimes you have to bend the rules for personal advantage, just to get by these days." In comparison, though, a solid majority of the nondonors (56 percent) buy that perspective. More than 6 out of 10 who attend but do not support a church also accept such a philosophy. Undoubtedly, the moralizing role of the church grates on the nerves—and, perhaps, the conscience—of many adults who prefer to ignore inconsistencies in their thinking and behavior about issues that relate to morality and personal values.

> **"NOT TO GIVE TO THOSE IN NEED WHAT IS TO YOU SUPERFLUOUS IS AKIN TO FRAUD." AUGUSTINE**

The question at hand is not whether a Christian church should have—and promote—a perspective about morals and values. No one could reasonably argue that teaching and modeling biblical morality, ethics and values are not core priorities of a Christian church. The point is that there is a noteworthy relationship between the moral stands taken by churches and the ability of a church to raise money for ministry. There is a price to pay for championing a consistent, biblical moral view.

Absolutes in a Relativistic World

A growing majority of Americans do not believe in moral or ethical absolutes. Most adults currently believe that decisions of what is right or wrong depend on the circumstances and the person who must make such a judgment call. Churches that teach a belief in absolute moral truths are viewed by increasing numbers of Americans as closed-minded, old-fashioned, unrealistic and fanatical.

It is both amazing and frightening to discover the few differences in the perspectives of church donors and nondonors when it comes to perspectives about the existence of absolute truth. Clearly, the Bible teaches that specific, God-ordained truths are eternal and undeniable. Nevertheless, most church supporters, like their nondonor counterparts, reject the existence of absolute truths.

This sweeping abandonment of absolute truth helps to explain why the church struggles to convince people about the importance of moral integrity, the significance of biblical values and the need to support the church in its work.

Lifestyles

Perspectives related to lifestyles highlight some of the areas in which churches are missing the mark in developing their people—and, at the same time, losing opportunities for raising money for ministry. Notice, for instance, that a majority of people—both church donors and nondonors—believe that the primary purpose of life is self-satisfaction. This perception is even more pronounced among the nondonors, and provides insight into why many of them do not take the church seriously enough to invest their money in its efforts.

After studying several dozen lifestyle endeavors, our research produced few noteworthy distinctions between church donors and nondonors. In fact, among the elements we examined, the only real differences were that donors are slightly more likely to read books and slightly more likely to volunteer their time. Otherwise, the lifestyles of donors and nondonors are nearly identical (apart from involvement in religious activities).

This striking similarity of lifestyles—that is, applying faith principles to daily activity—raises the question about whether exposure to the typical church ministry makes any difference in people's lives. If the answer is no—and it is possible to muster an impressive array of statistics that point to this conclusion—then many serious challenges are unavoidable.

Are churches doing what they exist, biblically, to do? Have American churches lost their ability to effectively communicate and influence in today's culture? Should churches that have no apparent positive influence on people's lives continue to take up space, energy and money? Should people even consider giving money to ministries that are not agents of personal and cultural transformation? Given the many alternatives people have for donations, is the typical church a competitive force?

For millions of adults, participating in church life is not helping to transform them from people of the world to people of the Kingdom. If their church experience is not playing a significant role in shaping (or reshaping) them, then it stands to reason that many people lack a compulsion to donate to a church. If the church experience is not a major, transformational reality, then it is easy to imagine adults attending a church solely because it temporarily satisfies the felt need for spiritual pursuit and development. They might also attend because it offers a sense that a truce with God has been reached, or perhaps because people believe that once the church generates sufficient personal benefits for them (e.g., relationships, knowledge, comfort, material assistance), then they will begin to return some of the benefit through financial support.

The Lessons of Psychographics

In summary, then, we found that in many areas the attitudes and values of donors are identical to those of nondonors. Among the few aspects that distinguish donors from nondonors are their greater degree of support for the traditional family, their more pronounced interest in religion, their comparative rejection of liberal social policy stands and lower levels of change and turbulence in their lives. These distinctions are useful toward conceiving means of communicating, ministering and positioning a church's ministry in ways that not only help people on a daily basis, but that also facilitate the ability to raise money for effective church work.

Theolographics™

Until recently, the term "theolographics" did not exist. I coined the term after spending countless hours studying people's lifestyles, thought patterns, behavioral patterns and spiritual composure, arriving at the conclusion that we cannot truly understand people's donor behavior until we understand their spirituality.

Calling the range of religious thoughts, perceptions, practices and theological beliefs "religiosity" or "spirituality" is not a sufficiently accurate reflection of the content of the range of measures we use to dig into a person's understanding of, and involvement with, all aspects of religion and spirituality.

As shorthand for a more holistic understanding of all these matters, I began describing this wealth of input as "theolographics," and the term stuck. Just as demographics relates to people's socioeconomic characteristics, and psychographics refers to people's values, attitudes and lifestyles, so theolographics refers to a comprehensive outlook of people's religious beliefs, experiences, expectations and practices.

In a previous examination of donor behavior (*The Mind of the Donor*), I described the importance of theolographics for those who wish to predict a person's likelihood of giving or to gain insight into a person's possible giving pattern. Of all the measures typically used by researchers and social analysts to understand behavior, theolographics has the strongest relationship with a person's likelihood of donating to churches and other nonprofit organizations.

Theolographic variables generally have a much greater level of influence on giving than do all but a handful of demographic attributes, and a much greater influence than any of the psychographic elements we have tested. Yet in spite of the demonstrated significance of these factors, they tend to be ignored by fund-raisers, marketers and by many religious leaders who are involved in raising funds for ministry activity.

Believing Precedes Giving

Simply put, the more firmly an adult embraces fundamental Judeo-Christian principles, the more likely he or she is to donate to a church. Donors are more certain about the existence and the reliability of God; they are more likely to consider the church to be relevant to their own lives and needs; they more commonly think of affiliating with a church as a positive, beneficial relationship; and they are more apt to believe that the Christian faith has all the answers to leading a successful life.

The differences do not end there. Donors are also more likely to exhibit a stronger belief in the reality of sin, to accept the truth and relevance of the Ten Commandments and to believe that the pursuit of personal spiritual development is an important and necessary component to meaningful living. They are also more likely to view the church's efforts at raising money as a means toward enabling the church to provide ministry services than to characterize it as a self-serving act. In other words, donors are more likely than nondonors to align themselves theologically with traditional Judeo-Christian thinking and teaching. Nondonors, although not wholly heretical, are consistently more likely to embrace views that conflict with Scripture.

Adults who attend church regularly but do not donate to their church are clearly different from those who attend regularly and give. The differences are revealing.

On the one hand, those who attend church but do not give hold opinions that are strikingly similar to the giving attenders about matters such as the certainty of being able to trust God in a crisis, the importance of a church connection, the belief that Christianity provides what it takes to help one live successfully, the necessity of pursuing spiritual development and the power of prayer.

On the other hand, we found that the attending nondonors have significantly different perspectives about the relevance of the Christian faith, the relevance of their church and what constitutes an acceptable level of emphasis on fund-raising by churches. This means that those who attend but do not give are still in the "seeker" mode. They are searching for greater meaning, purpose and direction in life, but have not discerned how church-based Christianity can be sufficiently personal, practical and relevant to meet their needs.

Owning the Ministry

My research also confirmed a powerful link between giving money and giving time to a church. In short, the best donors are the church's volunteers. Volunteers are the people who have the highest stake in the church's ministry; their commitment to the community of faith transcends merely attending and observing the ritual on Sunday mornings. Volunteers have invested a piece of themselves in the ministry.

We discovered that often people donate time and energy first, then make serious financial commitments to the church later. Why? Because after becoming an active part of the faith community and its ministry, people not only have a vested interest in funding the work, but also truly own the ministry. People who become active participants through teaching, serving as lay leaders, participating in a small group, leading a Sunday School class, volunteering to help or participating in a 12-step group through the church are about 50 percent more likely to donate funds to the church than are people who are not involved in any of those ways.

Yet another indicator of owning ministry is reflected by the fact that adults who are exposed to Christian media are significantly more likely to donate to their church than are those who do not pay attention to Christian books, magazines, radio or television. On average, nondonors are about 80 percent less likely to have exposure to Christian media than are church donors.

Compelled by God or Humans?

In exploring people's theological views, we might divide these perspectives into four major dimensions: (1) views about the Bible and its teachings, (2) views about deity and the Trinity, (3) perspectives about salvation and forgiveness (4) and insights into supernatural power.

Realize that America is the most Bible-saturated nation on earth. More than 9 out of 10 adults own a Bible. What these owners of God's Word know about its contents is another matter.[4] When it comes to supporting a church financially, and what the Bible says about this matter, Bible knowledge is a delineating factor between those who do and those who do not contribute to their church financially. The gap between these two segments is unusually wide. The essence of the difference is that donors are more likely to take the Bible at face value than are most nondonors.

Those who believe the Bible can be interpreted literally have a deeper sense of responsibility to donate to a church than do those who believe the Bible is a good work but must be interpreted with caution and, sometimes, skepticism. Naturally, people who believe the Bible is God's Word are much more likely to donate to a church than are those adults who view the Bible as a useful but noninspired volume, or as simply a man-written book of religious ideas and suggestions.

Adults who do not donate to their church tend to be considerably more ignorant of Scripture's contents. This seems like a classic chicken-egg dilemma—i.e., which comes first, knowing the Bible and what it teaches about stewardship or giving as a matter of faith, where faith is a precursor to gaining extensive biblical knowledge regarding material resources? My reading of the situation is that many people sitting in the pews choose not to give to their church because they assume the pulpit pleas for money are simply human demands for resources, without a biblical underpinning.

To put this in context, recognize that most adults do not believe that the Bible is to be taken literally. Therefore, many of the teachings it contains are treated more as suggestions than as inviolable truths that ought to season one's life or that bring serious consequences to those who consciously ignore those teachings. Interestingly, we find that adults who attend church but do not donate have a considerable storehouse of biblical knowledge, but they feel little compulsion to give because they neither take the Bible literally nor sense the uniqueness of Christianity. The bottom line, then, is that they possess neither a true ownership of the Christian faith nor a sense of urgency about the mission of Christianity.

The Nature of God

People's perspectives about deity also influence their church-giving habits. Church donors differ radically from nondonors in terms of their respective views about the nature of God, the resurrection of Christ, Jesus' second coming and the notion that Christ made mistakes.

These findings are of immense importance toward comprehending why some people donate to their church and others do not. In essence, much of the reason may relate to the depth of each segment's acceptance of God, Jesus Christ and the Holy Spirit as real, eternal, omnipotent and loving entities. We know, beyond doubt, that millions of Americans who attend church on any given Sunday are not truly Christians. We also know that millions of Americans attend church for reasons that do not require them to accept Christianity's theological truths. Consequently, many of these people feel no obligation to finance the ministry, because they are not sold out to the fundamental theological truths of the Church.

Think about the implications of these distinctions. Among many who attend church but do not give money, the feeling is that salvation can be attained in ways other than relying upon the grace of God through the person of Jesus Christ. Similarly, refuting the likelihood of judgment by God eliminates the natural desire to worship God or express personal gratitude to Him through giving to His Church. These nondonors tend to minimize the nature and significance of God. Large percentages of them actually believe that Christ committed sins, that God cannot forgive all sins and that there is a universal means of salvation apart from Christ.

Salvation and Stewardship

One of the core distinctives of the Christian Church is its position regarding personal salvation: what it is, how to achieve eternal salvation and the implications of having or not having such a state of permanent peace with God. Church donors are much more likely than nondonors to accept God's grace as the only means to forgiveness, to believe that non-Christians will be consigned to hell and to believe God can forgive any and all sins, as appropriate.

Interestingly, we also learned that born-again Christians are more than twice as likely as nonbelievers to donate to a church. Almost two-thirds of all Christians donate to a church; only one-quarter of non-Christians follow suit. Is this surprising? Not really; you would expect those who have committed their lives to following Jesus to give freely of their worldly riches to be obedient to Him. What is surprising is that one-third of all born-again Christians do *not* donate money to their church. Another spin on these figures is that only one out of every four non-Christians donates to a church (and remember that we are talking about any level of giving, not just tithing). This is significant in light of our research which demonstrates that roughly half the adults who attend church services are not Christians.

The research also confirms that people's giving is related to the denominational affiliation and size of the church they attend. The larger the church people attend, up to about 500 people, the more likely they are to donate funds to the church. Half the adults who attend small churches give money, while 7 out of 10 adults who go to churches consisting of 500 or more people provide financial support to their churches. Denominationally, Protestants were slightly more likely than Catholics to donate to their church (53 percent versus 47 percent). In striking contrast, only one out of every seven Jews gives money to his or her synagogue. That suggests that Jews are just one-third as likely as Christians to donate to their religious center.

Within Protestantism giving varies by denomination. The people most likely to give are those aligned with the Assemblies of God (60 percent of those who attend these churches give money to them), Churches of Christ (61 percent) and Presbyterian churches (63 percent). Those associated with the Episcopal church are the least likely to give (46 percent). Giving at levels that fall within these extremes are people affiliated with nondenominational churches (59 percent), Lutherans (58 percent), Methodists (56 percent), Mormons (50 percent), Baptists (48 percent) and Pentecostal churches (47 percent).

The Lessons of Theolographics™

Not surprisingly, the chief discovery drawn from theolographics, in relation to church giving, is this: The more convinced people are of the veracity and relevance of biblical insights and the importance of the personal application of those insights, the more consistent and generous they are in their support of the church's ministry efforts.

The challenge, then, is perhaps little more than discovering how the church can effectively become an agent of transformation in a person's life. Clearly, efforts to get a person to donate more consistently and more generously are futile unless the church has prepared the person for spiritual growth. The more spiritual growth people experience, the more likely they are to "own" the ministry and assume personal responsibility for the church's financial needs.

Notes

1. The data on which this is based come from a trio of nationwide surveys conducted by Barna Research Group, Ltd. among adults from July 1995 through July 1996. Those surveys involved interviews about giving behavior by talking to more than 3,000 adults randomly selected from the 48 contiguous states.
2. In this book, as in all our research, I use four generational categories to describe American adults. Baby busters are the youngest group, 68 million strong, and include the people born between 1965 and 1983, inclusive. Baby boomers are the nation's largest generation ever, presently encompassing about 78 million individuals. Boomers were born between 1946 and 1964. Builders are those born between 1927 to 1945; about 44 million of them remain. The older generation, known simply as seniors, include about 40 million adults, all of whom were born in 1926 or earlier.
3. The findings of this research were revealed in our report *The Mind of the Donor*. That study described information pertaining not just to donations to churches, but also to monetary contributions made to any nonprofit organization.
4. Current information regarding people's Bible knowledge and reading habits can be found in *The Index of Leading Spiritual Indicators* by George Barna (Dallas, Tex.: Word Publishing, 1996); and in Barna's bimonthly newsletter, *The Barna Report*, published by Word Ministry Resources, Waco, Tex., 1-800-933-9673.

4

Why People Give

"DONORS DON'T GIVE TO INSTITUTIONS.
THEY INVEST IN IDEAS AND PEOPLE IN
WHOM THEY BELIEVE."

G. T. SMITH

In this age of cynicism, it is easy to draw pejorative conclusions about people's motives for doing good deeds, but not have any basis for those conclusions. As a case in point, many social commentators have declared, without the benefit of empirical evidence to support their claims, that people donate money primarily to receive tax deductions. Another common charge is that most donors give to assuage their guilt about having so much while most people have so little. Indeed, conventional wisdom explains that in these times of wanton selfishness, greed and self-interest, people have totally abandoned their sense of caring about the human condition and have lost their ability or will—or both—to do the right thing for the right reasons.

The good news is that the pundits are only partially correct. Although most people who donate significant amounts of money to nonprofit organizations do take the permissible charitable deductions on their income tax forms, we have discovered that relatively few Americans give primarily to receive the deductions. The pundits, however, are correct in stating that donors do not always have pure motives; millions of donors are greatly concerned about the personal, tangible benefits they will receive in some way, at some time, from their generosity.

On balance, though, we have no reason to castigate Americans for their giving. The majority of adults who give money to nonprofit organizations, including to churches, are not driven solely by self-interest and the hidden hope of personal gain or delayed gratification. Most people who give away money have altruistic motivations in their hearts. This is especially true among those who give to churches.

As skeptical, cynical, discouraged, unfulfilled and restless as the American people might be, we also remain a rather generous population. No other nation on the face of the earth gives away as much money as do Americans. The fact that the brunt of their giving is received by churches also sends an important message about why they give as much as they do, as often as they do and to the recipients they support.

Why People Give Away Money

Seeking to enter the heads and hearts of Americans is a complex and confusing endeavor. Although social scientists, marketers, theologians and journalists like to dissect a specific group and pronounce the discovery of the explanation for a set of behaviors, perceptions or motivations, reality is rarely so simple or clear as those explanations suggest. I usually find people's decisions and actions riddled with inconsistencies and lack of logic. Few people seem to have successfully married the head and the heart to emerge with a fully predictable, internally consistent, purely logical and totally loving mixture. What we usually get is a bizarre concoction of understanding, desire, good will, morality and values, resulting in a set of behaviors that are only partially consistent.

Discerning the motivations underlying people's giving to charities and to churches, then, is no simple task. Because most Americans (i.e., those from the boomer, builder and seniors generations) have a strong distaste for contradictions and mystery, we tend to analyze the environment and draw black and white conclusions. An honest appraisal of the reasons for donating money, though, results in the following conclusions:

- Most people have never fully or critically thought through their charitable giving or what motivates them at the deepest level.
- Most adults give to nonprofit organizations for several reasons; no single reason adequately describes what moves the typical person to give away his or her money.
- A person who gives to a variety of nonprofits may donate to each of those entities for different reasons. In each case, the reasons are germane specifically, and perhaps uniquely, to the particular organization to which he or she is giving.
- Once a person donates to an organization, he or she is likely to continue to donate to the entity, or to have an openness to donating to it, for a long time. In most cases, it takes a scandal

(or allegation of wrongdoing), a personal inst
tentional) or a statement or action that radicall
core belief of the donor to cause that giver to
ing organization or ministry.[1]

These descriptions do not paint the most flattering picture of donors. This is not the profile of bad people, however, but a portrait of people who are so busy or perplexed that they have not maximized the experience of donating. Nevertheless, they give and give and give, and have a generally positive feeling about their participation in making the world a better place through their sharing.

Basic Motivations

Donors are usually driven by a combination of several motivations, regard-less of the recipients of their donations. By far the most important of those is the reputation or credibility of the nonprofit organization (NPO). Unless donors are comfortable with the trustworthiness of an otherwise viable NPO, they will withhold their money—no matter how worthy the cause, how many endorsements the organization received or how many appeals the donor received from the agency. This demand for overt credibility and trustworthiness stands as the most imperative condition an NPO must sat-isfy prior to receiving a hearing, serious consideration and eventually a donation.

Also of importance in moving a donor to support an organization are the endorsements of respected persons known personally by the donor. Although people often rely upon their friends for recommendations, the downturn in confidence in other people has undermined even word-of-mouth endorsements as an indisputable source of insight. Word-of-mouth recommendations remain an important but imperfect means of raising peo-ple's awareness of a charitable group and an integral element in confirming a potential donor's inclination to give to a specific NPO.

Recommendations from celebrities and other high-profile people no longer have the magnetism and influence such statements of support had years ago. Celebrity endorsements still have the ability to grab donors' attention and make them aware of the organization, but such endorsements rarely have the power, by themselves, to cause people to give their money to the endorsed entity. Our research indicated that most donors believe all celebrity endorsements are paid endorsements, and thus have considerably less credibility and influence.

Another important motivation for giving is having had one or more pos-itive, personal experiences with the NPO. In view of our increasing skepti-

regarding people's recommendations—even those from friends and
.ended family members—more and more people are relying heavily upon
personal encounters with an organization as a primary determinant of fund
worthiness. In the same way a majority of adults believe the only things you
can trust or believe are those you have personally experienced, many donors
now contribute only to those organizations with which they have personally
been involved in some manner. Involvement may mean working as a volunteer, being the beneficiary of services rendered by the NPO or having knowledge of the NPO's efforts from someone who received them firsthand.

A couple of comparatively unimportant reasons for giving to NPOs are
persuasive marketing and promotional activity, and self-evaluation of the
organization's influence and work quality. Donors mistrust the former
because they assume such marketing will put the best face or most positive
spin on the NPO and its efforts, perhaps to the point of misleading people.
Americans have a healthy skepticism of marketing, assuming that professional marketers labor to cleverly and convincingly manipulate the perceptions, emotions and desires of the public.

Meanwhile, most donors do not accept reports from the NPO about the
quality of its work at face value because they assume the organization is
more interested in building a good image than in providing an honest read
on its own performance. A donor may be introduced to a potentially viable
recipient of funds by the organization's own public relations, but most
donors today are savvy—and wary—enough to look for other, more objective indicators of performance quality.

We also discovered that most donors distinguish giving to churches
from giving to nonchurch nonprofits. A person's motivations for giving to
churches often vary from the motivations for giving to nonchurch charities—even when a church and a nonchurch entity being supported by the
donor are dedicated to achieving the same outcomes.

Why People Give Money to Churches

Overall, six primary motivations compel a person to give money to a
church. Although most churches need not trigger all six motivations to
inspire a person to donate to the church, the more of these reasons the
church can stimulate, the better are its chances of receiving an initial gift
and of having that person develop into a long-term supporter.

One of the ways giving to churches differs from that of giving to other
nonprofits is that church donors are more likely to have firsthand awareness of the influence and efforts of the church and to encounter favorable
feedback about the ministry of the church. Such feedback might come from
others within the church or from people in the community who had been

positively influenced by the church's ministry.

Church donors are also more likely than are other people to interpret the laudable work done by their church as an indication that the organization is reliable and trustworthy. Amazingly—although understandably—churches, like every other nonprofit entity, must prove themselves credible before donors will support them. No longer is it automatically assumed that a church does good work and that it is trustworthy. As we prepare to enter the new millennium, churches must gain respect the "old-fashioned way"—that is, they must earn it.

An adult who is aware of a church might choose to donate to it for six dominant reasons. We will delve into each reason.

Shared Cause

More than 9 out of 10 adults who give money to churches said they do so because they are convinced the church believes in and stands for the same things as the donor. This notion of having a shared cause is virtually indispensable in attracting donations.

Establishing a sense of a shared cause is somewhat more difficult for a church than for other NPO's because the church must have "the right beliefs" about several different theological and social criteria. For example, pleasing positions about issues of importance to the potential donor—such as the role of women in ministry, abortion and homosexuality—may be cancelled out by having positions that differ from those of the potential supporter about core issues such as divorce, prayer in schools, evangelistic strategy and tithing.

> **DONORS LOOK FOR ORGANIZATIONS WITH WHICH THEY HAVE A HEART CONNECTION—A SHARED CAUSE THAT MAKES THE ORGANIZATION A COMPELLING RECIPIENT OF FUNDS.**

In contrast, it is generally easier for nonchurch charities to win donors because they only have to be recognized as addressing a cause of major interest to the person and to be on the "right side" of that cause. This makes matters more complicated for a donor who is trying to determine whether or not a church—even one he or she attends regularly—is truly "worthy" of his or her financial contributions.

Although some church leaders seek to minimize the importance of informing people about the core beliefs and principles for which the church stands, our data about stewardship practices firmly intimate that adults are unable to feel emotionally, philosophically and theologically aligned with the church unless such elements are easily accessible.

The importance of being positioned as a cause with which the donor resonates poses a major challenge to most churches. Our research shows that few churched adults think of the church they attend as cause driven or as representing a cause. Even among those who say their church is a cause-driven organization, a majority of them describe their church's "cause" in generic, bland terms, such as the "cause of religion" or the "cause of Christ." Such vague, broad "causes" are unlikely to inspire people to become so focused, passionate and involved in the cause that they will also part with their money to support the church's work in the pursuit of the cause.

Ministry Efficiency

Nobody likes to throw away money, especially money that is being donated. Four out of five church donors said they will give only if they are persuaded the church uses people's money carefully and wisely. In the eyes of most donors, this is a fair requirement. Just as the typical church exhorts donors to manage God's money wisely and efficiently, so the typical church donor expects the church to model that behavior in how it utilizes the funds it receives for ministry.

Operating efficiently is particularly important for churches because donors are regularly on site: They can see how their money is used and will rapidly evaluate whether or not the church uses donations carefully. Donors rarely have a firsthand look at the work carried out by the nonchurch NPO's they support. In those instances, donors warily rely upon an efficiency evaluation offered by the NPO's executives, usually delivered through appeal letters, annual reports or presentations at special events. Churches, though, are exposed: It is difficult to hide inefficiency or ineptitude from donors because the evidence of such inefficiency is in plain view every week.

> **CHURCH DONORS NEED CONTINUAL EVIDENCE THAT THEY ARE GIVING MONEY TO A FINANCIALLY EFFICIENT MINISTRY.**

The congregation's expectation of operational efficiency means that most American churches must rethink how they interact with their constituency. In almost all the churches I studied, pastors and staff assumed the congregation would either accept the church's level of efficiency without scrutiny or complaint, or those who examine the church's operations would conclude it operates efficiently.

Unfortunately, tens of thousands of church leaders are ministering with a false sense of security. My interviews with donors revealed that many of the current donors—and a large proportion of the regular attenders who do not give anything to the church—assume that any donor-funded organization—yes, even their church—is of average or below average efficiency unless they encounter convincing contrary evidence. In other words, the church must prove to donors that it uses donations in a careful and parsimonious manner. Providing tangible evidence—such as detailed financial reports, comparative reports and cost-per-outcome figures—speaks volumes to donors who might otherwise assume the church is a muddler.

Ministry Influence

Three trends make evidence of ministry influence a critical condition for raising funds. The first of those is the desire of baby boomers to change the world in their own image, leaving a lasting mark on the world that reflects their values. The second is the tendency of baby busters to intensely invest themselves in causes they believe will enhance the quality of life.

The third trend is a common result of aging. As people reach their fifties, large numbers of them discover they have reached their career pinnacle and have achieved most of the significant goals they had set for their lives. The most unsettling discovery, though, is that these successes have been relatively unsatisfying. That realization often leads to a new quest for their remaining years, a quest to live a life of significance rather than a life of selfishness. This life-stage shift influences many aspects of life, including the way these people donate funds to organizations.

> **"THE ONLY RIGHT STEWARDSHIP IS THAT WHICH IS TESTED BY THE RULE OF LOVE." JOHN CALVIN**

Taken together, these generational differences intersect to indicate that many donors are searching for a channel of influence. One of the many paradoxes of our era juxtaposes people's innate desire to do what is morally or spiritually appropriate with the American norm of doing what is most culturally defensible. On the one hand, church donors want to do what is right by giving to the causes and ministries that should be supported simply because they are making the Christian faith tangible by doing God's work. On the other hand, even the most worthy of causes, done from the most pure motives, will fail to generate sufficient operating funds unless it can somehow convince potential donors that lives are being changed in sufficient numbers, that world conditions are being notably improved or that other significant outcomes are being produced in response to money donated to the church.

People no longer give to the church simply because it is the church. Some analysts say this is a direct outgrowth of teaching people to think like

good stewards: Only invest in people or organizations that produce justifiable outcomes. Other analysts proclaim this is an outgrowth of secular
thinking: People's behavior is driven by a selfish need to leave a personal
mark, rather than by a desire to do what is culturally, morally or humanis-
tically appropriate. For whatever reason, the outcome is this: Unless a
church can demonstrate that the world is being sufficiently and appropriately changed for the better by its ministry, an increasing number of donors
won't place the church on their short list of preferred fund recipients.

> **PEOPLE NO LONGER GIVE TO THE CHURCH SIMPLY
> BECAUSE IT IS THE CHURCH. THE CHURCH MUST
> PROVE IT IS WORTHY OF DONATIONS THROUGH
> THE MARK IT LEAVES ON THE WORLD.**

Among pastors, the old wisdom about giving was, "We don't have to
persuade people to support the church; that's God's job." The new wisdom
is, "We must effectively convey to our people what we stand for, how we
minister and what difference it makes in people's lives." The new wisdom
is not a repudiation of the old perspective, but a recognition that times have
changed and we must do a greater share of the work to prepare people to
sense God's direction in their lives. Simply waiting for God to touch people's hearts with a desire to give money to the church may sound more spiritual, but the new wisdom is certainly a reflection of practical theology,
based on James 4:2,3: "You do not have because you do not ask God. When
you ask, you do not receive, because you ask with wrong motives, that you
may spend what you get on your pleasures."

Today, four out of five church supporters actively search for evidence
that their money has made a difference in people's lives. Now here's the
rub. Most churches are struggling to trigger this motivation for giving
because relatively few churches periodically, quantitatively and objectively
measure their ministry influence. In an age of consumer skepticism, organizational excellence and virtually infinite choices, churches cannot afford
to risk reliance upon people's assumptions and good will.

The fund-raising environment is a competitive one, and churches must
learn how to compete in that milieu or face the consequences. Naturally,
this is not the way we wish things were, but that is the nature of the world
in which we live. The choices are clear: Become a "humble self-promoter"
(i.e., tell the story of positive influence honestly, humbly and emphasize
God's blessings) or lose donations to other organizations (including many
parachurch ministries) who are more proficient at making their transformational influence known to the donor public.

An Urgent Need

Whether you like it or not, most donors have fallen prey to the "crisis of the day" mentality. We have all been so shocked, so horrified, so moved—and so inundated—with crises occurring around the corner and around the world that fund-raisers regularly rely upon heart-wrenching tales of human hardship to raise money. Organizations that specialize in fund-raising have become more sophisticated and have learned how to communicate captivating messages about urgent needs to people likely to have a soft spot in their hearts for such emergencies.

Unfortunately, given the magnitude of the pain, suffering and injustice throughout the world, the persistent presence of severe crises always merits our attention and our assistance. Because most donors want their giving to make a difference in people's lives, to maximize the good the donor can do, to be part of something special and unique or to make a tangible difference in the world, credible and timely crisis-alleviation appeals from nonchurch nonprofits are often irresistible. Because most donors have a limited supply of funds from which they make their donations, some need or opportunity to which they otherwise would have given is likely to be replaced. The organization experiencing the most serious, most urgent and most convincing need wins the donation.

Most church leaders think of two kinds of fund-raising: fund-raising for emergency needs and fund-raising for perpetual needs. Victims of floods, wars, famine and health epidemics fit the former category. The church owns the second category. If there truly ever was a distinction in the minds of donors between emergency and perpetual needs, we now know that such a delineation is no longer relevant in contemporary giving. These days donors evaluate all potential needs in relation to the same criteria.

Our data suggest that a majority of church donors (6 out of 10) admit they are more likely to give when they become aware of an urgent need, whether that need emanates from their church or from some other organization. Although many people give to their church regularly, millions of adults either upgrade their level of giving or give more consistently when they know that a significant and compelling need requires funds immediately. (This does not necessarily include a building campaign, which churches describe as a need "above and beyond" people's regular giving, and which is therefore interpreted by millions of church donors as a "luxury" rather than a necessity.)

Communicating the ongoing financial requirements of the church as urgent ministry needs is a major paradigm shift for most church leaders. I found that most church leaders expect people to give regularly and generously. In a cultural context in which such expectations are no longer reasonable, I also discovered that the churches most effective at fund-raising are those that are most consistent and compelling in communicating the needs the church wishes to address. These churches abandon the ancient, comfortable assumptions about people's goodheartedness and inevitable support in favor of a realistic perspective and set of behaviors based on the knowledge that to an ever-increasing number of people, the church is just one more organization reaching out its hand and asking for money.

> **CHURCH FUND-RAISING HAS BECOME THE ART OF HONESTLY AND CONVINCINGLY DESCRIBING THE MANY, ONGOING NEEDS OF THE CHURCH IN TERMS OF THE URGENCY OF THOSE NEEDS.**

Fund-raising in the church, as everywhere, has become a specialized art. It takes a keen understanding of the donor audience and talent in communicating to be an effective fund-raiser. The task is complicated in the church world by the extreme caution fund-raisers must use to ensure that all they do is ethical. As much as analysts and journalists like to suggest that unethical fund-raising is detectable a mile away, the truth is that sometimes only a fine line is discernable between raising money by manipulating people's perceptions or emotions and being able to authentically and honestly convey an urgent need deserving of prayer and generosity. Knowing how to blend the communication of such needs with the notion of regular and generous giving to a seemingly stable institution is an art the leaders of the most effective money-raising churches have intellectually, emotionally and spiritually have perfected over a prolonged period.

Personal Benefit
Many people give to their church because they wish to express their gratitude for what the church has done in their own lives or in the lives of people close to them. In some cases, we also found that a donor may support a church because he or she believes the church will eventually make a major difference in the life of the donor or of those who are significant to the donor.

In some cases, people were giving to their church because it was the place through which they came to personally know Jesus Christ and gain an assurance of eternal salvation. In other cases, people were supporting the church because the leaders had prayed for healings or other personal needs of the donor or their family and friends; the church had become a place of stability and comfort for the donor; the church had provided the donor with an outlet for his or her spiritual gifts, which in turn gave the person a renewed sense of purpose and influence; or the donor believed that the church was providing the teaching, modeling and accountability needed to enable him or her to grow as a Christian.

Frequent but less common motivations for giving included hoped-for benefits that would emerge from the church and meet the donor's needs. Examples of such deferred expectations were the salvation of the donor's children; the church's willingness to pray for and befriend the donor when he or she became ill or aged; helping to alleviate poverty and physical hardship within the community; or providing an educational or youth ministry that might help others find peace, forgiveness or salvation through Christ.

> **MANY PEOPLE GIVE TO A CHURCH BECAUSE THEY HAVE RECEIVED IDENTIFIABLE BENEFITS FROM THE CHURCH, OR BECAUSE THEY HOPE THE CHURCH WILL PROVIDE CERTAIN BENEFITS TO THEM AND THEIR LOVED ONES IN THE FUTURE.**

Some church leaders have wrongly interpreted this motivation as being overly transactional (i.e., "I will give the church money after it gives me something of value"). Granted, some donors (typically those who give sparingly and infrequently) think and behave this way. I found that more often than not, though, those who give in response to (or in the hope of) getting something from the church had less selfish reasons for their generosity. Those who contribute to a church in recognition of how the church has satisfied a personal need are rarely giving to just "even the score with God and His people." As we probed the depths of this motivation, we discovered that the inspiration for such giving is gratitude and responsibility.

I was surprised to learn how many church leaders perceive giving borne of this motivation to be inappropriate or unbiblical; some go as far as to chastise donors for giving out of "selfish motives." Such is not necessarily the case, though; consider just how biblical such a motive is. Throughout His teaching and healing ministry, Jesus habitually taught a useful truth or performed a good deed for someone, then asked the recipient to demonstrate gratitude through an overt act of service to others.[2] Jesus was the catalyst of good works in others' lives. That did not minimize the importance or the influence of those good works done by those whom He had first served.

This Kingdom practice preceded the earthly ministry of Jesus. In Genesis 12, we read of God telling Abraham that He would bless Abraham and his descendants so that they, in turn, could be a blessing to others. Clearly, it was God's initiative; and clearly, God expected and accepted the efforts of Abraham and his family to make God's love real to others.

The harsh reality is that although we embrace Christ as both a Savior and role model, we remain human, committing sins and losing perspective every day. Sometimes we reflect our faith values and Christian principles by observing a need and meeting it, just as Jesus would have, without expecting recognition or reward. Other times we are the recipients of a good deed or convicting teaching, and we feel drawn to respond in an appropriate way. Responding to such positive influences is no less significant because of the context. We always have good reason to applaud people's appreciation for benefits received, or to joyfully accept gifts prompted by an appropriate sense of duty or obligation. Donations given in response to a benefit received may not seem as selfless or altruistic in nature as are gifts donated for purely emotional or spiritual reasons, but they are every bit as significant and justifiable.

Relationship with the Ministry

People do not like to give money based on a sense of guilt or mandate. They are willing to give, however, based on a sense of partnership in a meaningful ministry in which their financial assistance is integral to the health and vitality of the church. Six out of 10 adults said they give to their church out of a feeling of responsibility or moral obligation to the Christian community to which they belong and to the ministries in which they participate.

Our research showed that most people want a developing, ongoing relationship with their church. For some people, that relationship facilitates their donating to the ministry, while for others the relationship with the ministry is an end in itself. Consequently, we learned that some people who attend church believe that having a tangible relationship with the church is "absolutely necessary"; some describe it as "desirable but not necessary"; others think such a bond is "desirable but not likely to happen." Relationships with the church are more commonly a precipitant to giving among people who are first-time or small-sum donors, those who have limited economic means and people who volunteer their time to other charitable organizations besides the church.

> **MANY DONORS MUST FEEL A LEVEL OF OWNERSHIP OF THE MINISTRY BEFORE THEY WILL SUPPORT IT FINANCIALLY. CONSEQUENTLY, THEY NEED A SENSE OF "RELATIONSHIP" WITH THE CHURCH.**

The most interesting aspect of this line of inquiry, though, proved to be people's descriptions, in their own words, of what it meant for them to have a relationship with a church. In essence, this notion is very personal and idiosyncratic; there is no dominant model of a church-donor relationship. The only commonality is how important donors feel such relationships are in their link to the church.

We discovered several ways to understand what most people might look for in a relationship between the church and the church donor. The following brief descriptions convey the five most common perspectives we encountered.

1. *The donor is personally involved in the ministry or operations of the church.* People who served as a lay minister within the church's overall ministry, as a volunteer assisting with the church's operations, on the board of directors or other decision-making body or through other kinds of personal, hands-on interaction related to the church's ministry were the most likely to say they had a relationship and that it was meaningful to them. (In some cases, this sense of a personal stake was as simplistic as "membership" in the organization.) The speech of such people is peppered with phrases such as "my church" and "our ministry team" as indications of an emotional connection to the church. The easiest way to create a sense of relationship with donors is to get them into the trenches, intimately involved in the work of the organization.

2. *The church keeps the donor aware of what the church is doing.* Providing a steady and useful flow of information is considered by many church donors as a way of distinguishing "outsiders" from "insiders." The communications perceived to be relationship-building are those that are personalized and targeted to the people and activities most interesting to, or involving of, the donor. As in person-to-person relationships, the absence of current and meaningful information about what is happening in the lives of the parties involved stunts the health and growth of the relationship.

3. *The donor has developed significant ties with other church donors.* One of the secrets to building organizational loyalty is to persuade people who are already intensely loyal to the entity to bond with others who are interested in the organization. Frequently, the passion of the loyalists infects the curious, resulting in an ever-widening circle of loyalists. In this case, when a church attender discovers that some of his or her friends or other respected attenders are regular and generous donors to the work of the church, that attitude of generosity often affects the giving of the less committed supporter. This has the effect of building a dual-level commitment: loyalty to the church and loyalty to donor-friends in the church.

4. *The donor, or people significant to the donor, have benefited from the church's ministry.* If this sounds familiar, it may be because this

motivation was listed earlier as one of the primary reasons behind people's giving. We also learned, however, that some people perceive the help they or significant others have received from the church to be one way of establishing ongoing, significant relational ties. Just as Jesus healed people and they therefore felt a bond to Him afterward, many people perceive they have a relationship with a church after the church has served their needs in a tangible way.

5. *The donor feels a special connection to the church because of a mutual desire to advance a particular cause or idea.* Another case of deja vu. This, too, was listed as one of the dominant motivations for giving to a church, yet in this context the joint, intense commitment to a common cause may be viewed as part of a larger effort (i.e., establishing a long-term relationship).

Not surprisingly, many people seeking a relationship with the church as the predecessor to their giving are likely to give more quickly or more generously if two or more of these relational fuses are ignited. We also discovered that relational strategies vary in effectiveness. Relationships are most easily and significantly built with conservatives if they can be meaningfully involved in the ministry. In contrast, church people who hold liberal social and political views are more likely to develop a relationship based on an ideological or emotional connection with the principles, theology or activities championed by the church.

People who have never shown much, if any, inclination to support a church are often eased into regular giving by receiving some tangible assistance from the church. Young adults are less likely than their predecessors to consider direct involvement in ministry at the church to constitute a relationship with the church. Their expectations pertaining to church-donor relationships are more diverse than is true for any other age group, perhaps because many baby busters are still distilling the meaning of relationships in their lives and in society.

The Second Mile

Understanding what motivates people to support a church is invaluable, not only to raise funds for ministry, but also to get a handle on people's values, priorities and perceptual filter.

Our research also found two other valuable insights regarding motives for donating. First, the marketplace for donations has become so competitive and so diversified that it is no longer sufficient to stimulate just one or two of these motivations. The typical donor these days dismisses any organization—whether it is a church or some other kind of nonprofit—that does not *simultaneously trigger at least three of the six motivations* described earlier. We also found that the more of those motivations an organization triggers, the more likely that organization is to receive funding from the donor.

Second, I also noted that three particular motivations must usually be triggered before the potential donor gives a church serious consideration. Those three "must have" motivations are (1) resonance with the cause, (2) efficient use of donor funds and (3) effective application of those funds to human need. When those serve as a foundation, additional motivations can be exploited and usually exponentially enhance a church's standing in the eyes of potential donors.

Avoidable Diseases

It is helpful to know which approaches or strategies usually do not capture the hearts, minds and money of a potential donor to a church. Grasping this knowledge is particularly useful because some of these efforts are deceptive: that is, they may raise some money for the church, but what is overlooked or not recognized are the unfavorable realities or fallout created by the money-generating activities.

Be Careful in Sponsoring Events

For instance, nearly half of all churches raise money for ministry and operations through special events designated as fund-raisers. Nearly two-thirds of all church donors, however, said they generally find church fund-raising events unappealing, if not embarrassing. There are exceptions, of course. Many people identified specific events their church—or other churches—have sponsored as very positive experiences. Those events, however, seemed to be the exception to the rule. In general, people said they would gladly live without fund-raising events at their church.

People described several reasons events are disdained. Some potential donors complained about the predictable, routine and mundane nature of church events. Some people were protective of their time and said they would rather write a check than lose both time and money at an event in which they have limited interest. Other adults said they often feel manipulated by events, meaning they feel guilty if they do not participate or give, or they are left out of the church family if they avoid what is an otherwise exasperating experience. A few people noted they would rather have the money and effort committed to implementing the event be used for the outreach work of the church.

Can churches live without fund-raising events? Most could, without a doubt. We found that among the churches that sponsor fund-raising events, those endeavors usually represent less than 10 percent of the church's annual revenues. We also found that a majority of pastors said such events are typically a break-even proposition, at best. Many pastors said the true value of fund-raising events is not the money they raise, but the opportunities afforded people to become involved in the activity of the church and to develop new friendships and working relationships with other people in the congregation.

Self-Serving Ministry Can Backfire
The research also shows that appeals emphasizing the boomerang effect (i.e., exploiting the benefits that will be available to the donor from the church at some point in the future, when the donor will have a need for such benefits) have a limited attraction. Most donors feel uncomfortable investing in ministry simply because they can cash in that investment at a later date. To their credit, most donors think giving money today to exploit it tomorrow negates the good will and the other-centeredness of the donation. It is not so much the case that church donors do not want to support efforts that may have a boomerang effect; rather, they are indicating a discomfort with fund-raising strategies and communications that overtly identify the give-now-for-a-future-return kind of contribution. If they can capitalize on such a serendipitous reality, they are comfortable with it; giving with the desire to capitalize on it feels wrong.

Hyping Spiritual Reasons
Perhaps the most startling outcome of the research about people's motivations for church giving is how few of them give money to their church because they feel a spiritual compulsion to return to God what He has entrusted to them. Although many pastors define stewardship in this light, and discuss pledging, tithing and personal giving with a "God's trustee" perspective, Americans appear to be either hardened to, or ignorant of, the fundamental precepts of biblical stewardship. A core of adults accept this principle as truth and happily comply with it. As much as I can discern from the data, however, this group of stewards represent only about one out of every six or seven adults.

Millions of laity believe that when a church appeals for donations on the basis of biblical mandate, such appeals are little more than examples of ecclesiastical usury—a kind of sanctified extortion. Dig a bit beneath the surface, though, and you will probably find that this view does not reflect an informed, deeply held theological view. This outlook simply betrays people's ignorance of the Bible's teachings about stewardship and a concomitant unwillingness to embrace teachings that conflict with personal preferences or convictions.

Oddly, many people who give in consideration of spiritual realities believe that giving to the church will buy God's favor. In their eyes, transferring some of their personal wealth to the church coffers is an earthly investment that will reap tangible, automatic heavenly dividends. This undoubtedly relates to the fact that most Americans believe that our behavior on earth influences God's decision about our eternal security.[3]

Wise As a Serpent?

Yet another paradox emerges related to giving behavior. On the one hand, a chief motivation for giving is the perception that the church is efficient in how it utilizes incoming donations. On the other hand, less than 1 out of every 10 church donors ever asks for, or scrutinizes, a financial statement from the church to which donations are given. This condition is true not only in relation to church giving, but also for all charitable contributions. For years our research has underscored the fact that most donors to nonprofit organizations never ask for a financial statement.

I have discovered that in lieu of the facts, people operate on the basis of ignorance, instinct and blind trust. Many people who donate their hard-earned money to churches and other charitable organizations are not savvy about the use, protection and management of money. Millions of donors do not realize they *could* ask for and receive a financial statement. This ignorance is bolstered by the way most donors choose where to give their money: on the basis of feelings and emotions rather than on facts and thorough investigation. Ultimately, then, people are trusting that their instincts will lead them to make good decisions about how to support ministry and charitable endeavors.

When it comes to giving to churches, these tendencies are exaggerated. Most church donors have a limited idea of how their contributions are spent. They see the doors of the worship center open each weekend, hear the pastor deliver sermons and watch staff members and others provide prayer and counseling. They listen to overseas missionaries who are funded by the church and who report that they are changing lives around the world, and give a silent prayer of thanks that the youth of the church are engaged in Christian education activities. As a result, the underlying assumption is that the money donated is being used effectively and efficiently for ministry. After all, the church looks like and seems to be doing what a church is supposed to look like and be doing.

In a comparison we conducted between the financial statements of representative samples of churches and nonministry nonprofit organizations, we found that church statements are comparatively vague. Yet rarely do church donors request greater detail regarding the church's finances than that which is provided on the one-page documents available from the church.

Similarly, only a unique church attender studies and questions the church's annual budget, or the budgets of any of the program ministries under the church's umbrella. Instead, the typical church goer is flooded with church experiences and emerges with an emotional sense of the well-being of the ministry. Based on that feeling, the typical church donor determines whether or not the church is worthy of receiving his or her offerings throughout the year. Once a bond of trust and confidence is established—along with the satisfaction of other core motivations for giving—it takes a seismic shock wave to shatter the typical donor's confidence to the point where funding is withdrawn.

> **IT IS ONLY THE RARE CHURCH DONOR WHO HAS AN ACCURATE AND DETAILED UNDERSTANDING OF HOW THE CHURCH SPENDS ITS MONEY.**

Another corollary evolves in this church-donor relationship. Once a donor has made up his or her mind to support a church, the level of support usually changes very little over time. For example, people who tithe their income usually operate on automatic pilot once they make the decision to tithe. For them, the major question is not how much money to give away, but whether to give it all to their church. This question is relevant to more and more people because parachurch ministries, as well as a sea of other nonprofits, are hounding them for contributions.

The vast majority of adults (i.e., the 97 out of 100 who do *not* tithe) may be even more perplexing to church leaders. The evidence suggests that only a small proportion of church donors substantially change their donation levels from year to year. On average, church donors give less than 3 percent of their aggregate income to their church. In any given year, their donation level varies by less than one half of one percent of their annual income. Thus, in raising funds for the church, determining the level of giving is critical right from the start.

How People Groups Differ

Earlier we considered the primary motivations of donors. Naturally, a host of other reasons are considered for sharing resources with a church. As we explored the perspectives and giving behavior of donors according to their demographic and theolographic categories, though, we found that the most common differences between the various donor segments related to secondary, rather than primary, motivations. Even then, the distinctions in motivations for giving are limited. The bottom line is that most people give for the same reasons, although the relative importance of each reason in the final outcome of their giving may differ.

As you evaluate the potential giving abilities and inclinations of your congregation, keep in mind a few differences that might influence how you communicate, position or identify the needs of the church.

Gender Distinctions
Men are less likely than women to give on the basis of experiencing first-hand the effectiveness or efficiency of the church. Women, who tend to be much more hands-on in evaluating the ministry, are more likely to conduct their own on-site assessments of the ministry and to speak to other people about their personal experiences regarding the ministry before making a financial commitment. Men are more likely to seek facts that build a convincing argument regarding the church's ability to set worthy goals, meet those goals and perform its ministry duties efficiently.

Generational Distinctions
We observed a few notable generational differences. Baby busters (the group born between 1965 and 1983) are more likely to be motivated by the church's ministry reputation, the personal recommendations of friends and the convenience of giving. Compared to other generations, baby boomers (the segment born between 1946 and 1964) are more likely than others to be moved by a common cause and by gratitude for past help received from the organization. The older generations (i.e., builders and seniors) are driven by firsthand evidence of influence, feeling good about their support and endorsements by celebrities or other high-profile people.

Income Distinctions
Perhaps the biggest differences in motivations for giving are related to household income. The least affluent donors give to churches because of the emotional warmth and satisfaction that the act of giving provides them. Recommendations by other people and the ease of giving a donation also have a more positive effect on people from downscale households. Middle-income donors are more likely than others to give to a church because they or people close to them have been personally helped in some discernible way by the church.

The affluent are the most diverse in their motivations for donating. In comparison to people of lesser means, the affluent respond most positively to churches that have demonstrated sterling integrity and have developed a solid ministry program that supports their personal interests. In other words, they may be more compelled to donate to the church if it is focusing on alleviating needs that touch a soft spot in their hearts.

Faith Distinctions

Amazingly, we found that the sole significant difference in the giving motivations of born-again Christians and non-Christians was that Christians
were slightly less likely to view a tax deduction as a factor. Otherwise,
Christians and non-Christians were virtually identical in how they think
about and respond to church giving.

Self-Examination

Based on what we have learned from the research among church donors,
and from discussing those insights in this chapter, consider some key questions as you evaluate your church's proficiency at encouraging people to
support its ministry.

1. What is the specific cause your church is perceived to represent?
   Have you adequately positioned that cause as one that is shared
   by your supporters? How significant or compelling is that cause
   to the people who are your potential supporters? How professionally does the church represent that cause?
2. How carefully and wisely is every dollar spent by your church?
   When you compare the product of your church's spending to
   that of other public-service organizations, how do you rate?
   What specific efforts can you identify that demonstrate your
   desire to be frugal?
3. How many lives have been irrefutably changed in the past year
   as a direct result of your church's ministry? What magnitude of
   life change occurs as a result of exposure to your church? What
   have been the most effective ministries, programs and strategies? What is the balance between stories and facts in evaluating the church's ministry effectiveness?
4. When people think about the financial needs of your church, do
   they perceive the needs to be urgent or simply unending—that
   is, compelling or just a funding black hole? When people give to
   the church, are they giving to facilitate life change or merely to
   allow for organizational survival? What difference would it
   make if they did not give?
5. What personal benefits do your donors get from giving?
6. How well informed are your donors of (a) how their money is
   used? (b) what the church plans to do in the future? (c) the
   breadth of support the church receives from within the congregation? (d) how grateful the church's leaders are for the generous support the church receives?

Notes

1. For a more extensive examination of why people donate money to nonprofit orga-
    nizations, in general, see chapter 5 of *The Mind of the Donor* by George Barna
    (Oxnard, Calif.: Barna Research Group, Ltd., 1994).
2. As examples, consider Matthew 10:5-10; 19:16-22; Mark 1:29-31; 1:40-44; 5:1-20; and
    Luke 8:1-3.
3. In a series of nationwide surveys among adults during the past 15 years, we have
    found a trend toward an increasing percentage of people believing salvation is not
    a gift from God, made possible by and uniquely available through Christ's death
    and resurrection, but that salvation is earned by being and doing good. For a more
    expansive examination of such data, see *The Index of Leading Spiritual Indicators* by
    George Barna (Dallas, Tex.: Word Publishing, 1996).

chapter

5

A Biblical
Reorientation to Money

"ONE OF THE GREATEST MISSING TEACHINGS IN
THE AMERICAN CHURCH TODAY IS THE REMINDER
TO MEN AND WOMEN THAT NOTHING WE
HAVE BELONGS TO US."
GORDON MACDONALD

Many pastors tell me they believe they have adequately taught their congregations about the principles and responsibilities related to stewardship. Often, though, their congregants view things differently. Granted, they are not begging for more sermons or programs related to fund-raising or stewardship. The people, however, display an amazing level of ignorance about a topic on which they are supposedly well versed, and they are surprisingly open to learning more about their responsibilities before God.

One reason many pastors may underestimate people's openness to information about stewardship is that pastors typically are uncomfortable teaching and preaching about money matters. As a result, once a sermon or two has been delivered, the typical pastor is ready—and eager—to move on to more comfortable topics. Thus, analyzing people's understanding of stewardship principles may reflect a pastor's hope, bred by his discomfort with the subject, more than it describes the congregation's understanding of stewardship.

Our research shows that in spite of the occasional sermon or teaching about stewardship, most church people remain ill informed about the matter: they possess a general understanding of the idea that they should give, but they lack any depth of comprehension about why or how. What do they need to know?

In the remainder of this chapter we will touch upon some of the essential factors related to stewardship about which millions of church-going people are confused or uninformed. For each of these stewardship components I have identified some related Scripture passages. In some cases, the laity are likely to be familiar with the passage and, perhaps, even the principle. In most of these cases, however, Christians lack a holistic comprehension of how these passages and principles form a grand, seamless perspective of stewardship. Those believers who are able to get beyond proof texting and isolated insights into biblical sayings about matters of money and giving resources are able to grasp the concept of stewardship and are likely to become reliable stewards.

> **"WHEN IT COMES TO GIVING UNTIL IT HURTS, MOST PEOPLE HAVE A VERY LOW THRESHOLD OF PAIN." ANONYMOUS**

The following components and Scripture references are far from an exhaustive treatment of stewardship. Yet if the average believer understood even these fundamental truths, he or she would be far ahead of where the typical American Christian is today in comprehending stewardship. Use the outline that follows as a prototype on which you might base a prospective discovery process. This process can help you lead your people to a better understanding of the "big picture" of stewardship.

Personal Responsibility

Most adults within the church acknowledge that they have some degree of responsibility for the financial needs of the church. They assume, however, that the Bible does not prescribe a level of giving or a theology related to that responsibility. Consequently, their giving becomes random and emotional. Imagine what a difference it might make if most of your congregants both understood and believed that God expects each of us to fund the church generously, that He accepts no excuses for stinginess and that our lives are materially affected by our generosity.

Scriptural Perspective

- Luke 8:2,3 (the women in Jesus' entourage were widowed, but helped finance His ministry).

- Luke 16:10 (He will only trust us with much after we prove ourselves worthy with a little).
- Galatians 6:6 (we must support those who instruct us about the Bible).
- 3 John 8 (when full-time servants of Christ have needs, we should respond generously).

Giving as Worship

Stewardship is an act of worship; thus we should recognize that God is the owner of all things and all we do should be done by keeping His objectives, best interests and glorification in mind. When we give a gift to ministry efforts, it is our way of thanking Him for His love and generosity shown to us. Because we are called to worship Him by using every breath and every ounce of energy we possess—that is, to live our lives as a worship performance—the act of giving should be just another avenue for expressing our humility and love for Him.

"CHARITABLE GIVING SHOULD BE A SPIRITUAL, RATHER THAN ECONOMIC, DECISION. ECONOMICALLY, CHARITABLE GIVING NEVER PAYS." RONALD BLUE

Scriptural Perspective

- Genesis 28:16-22 (Jacob realized that all belongs to God, and used his tithe as a means of worship).
- Leviticus 22:17-22,29 (God deserves only the best of what we have to offer).
- 1 Corinthians 10:31 (giving, as in everything we do, should be done for God's glory).
- 2 Corinthians 9:12 (our giving is an expression of thanks to God).

God First

Most Christians believe that their first responsibility is to tend to their personal needs, then to give God a slice of the leftovers. The Bible, of course, provides an entirely different perspective. We are told in no uncertain terms that we are to give Him the first share of what we receive, and then to live off the rest.

Scriptural Perspective

- Deuteronomy 14:22,23 (revere Him by offering the first tenth of your wealth).
- Nehemiah 10:37-39 (God gets the first share of our reapings).
- Proverbs 3:9,10 (honor God with the firstfruit of your wealth).
- 1 Corinthians 16:2 (provide an offering on the first day of each week).

Trusting God

One of the reasons God asks us to be stewards is to test our willingness to truly trust Him. He does not need 10 percent or 20 percent or even 100 percent of His resources to be returned by us: He can get the job done with us or without us, through us or in spite of us. He was able to create the resources we oversee for Him in the first place, and He is abundantly capable of creating them anew or creating other means of having His plans accomplished. By entrusting resources to us, and giving us free reign in managing them, though, the priorities of our heart emerge clearly. His desire is that we will consistently demonstrate unbridled obedience and trust, and thus recognize our place in creation.

Scriptural Perspective

- 1 Kings 17:7-16 (the widow of Zarephath provided food for Elijah out of her depleted reserves).
- Luke 6:38 (give generously and it will be returned to you in like manner).
- 1 Timothy 6:17-19 (put your hope in God, not in your wealth).
- Hebrews 6:10 (God remembers our good efforts to help others).
- James 1:10 (the rich are lowly in position; their only hope is in God).

Attitude and Behavior

Christian development is largely a matter of refining our character, and stewardship plays a large role in that development. To become the kind of people who honor and reflect Christ, we must embrace some basic perspectives. For instance, we must realize we are stewards, entrusted with His goods, for His purposes, but with the freedom to squander His wealth. We are charged with giving His wealth generously to those who need it and those who, through their spiritual position and faithfulness, have earned it. We should distribute His resources joyously, even when we give sacrificial-ly—this should be a habit!

Part of our determination to give relentlessly, selflessly and generously is to set an example for all who have been blessed by Him. We should do this so that they, too, may enter into the joy, the privilege and the responsi-bility of sharing His resources with those in need and with those who have earned a share by serving as vocational ministers of the gospel.

> **"TO BE CLEVER ENOUGH TO GET A GREAT DEAL OF MONEY, ONE MUST BE STUPID ENOUGH TO WANT IT." G. K. CHESTERTON**

We Are Stewards
The American way of thinking is that we are self-sufficient and that we are responsible for all that we possess. The Bible provides a different perspec-tive, of course: that we are merely the overseers of God's earthly domain, responsible for taking care of His resources until Jesus returns. Getting peo-ple to understand and accept our role as managers rather than creators of wealth and resources is a crucial element toward encouraging good stew-ardship.

Scriptural Perspective

- Genesis 14:17-24 (Abraham acknowledged that his victory spoils were a gift from God).
- 1 Chronicles 29:14-18 (everything is God's; we watch over it on earth).
- Psalm 24:1,2 (everything belongs to God).
- Psalm 50:10-12 (God created, knows and owns everything that exists).
- 1 Corinthians 4:2 (Paul exhorted those being trusted to prove themselves faithful).

Giving Generously
One of God's expectations of His people is that we will reflect His generous blessings of us in the ways in which we seek to bless others. The model He provides to us is one of a loving Father who withholds nothing good from His children; He always takes care of their needs sufficiently. In like man-ner, we are to be generous in how we give His resources to address the needs of others.

Scriptural Perspective

- Deuteronomy 15:7-10 (give generously to those in need).
- Psalm 37:21 (generous giving is a mark of righteousness).
- Proverbs 11:24,25 (a generous giver will prosper).
- Luke 10:33-35 (the good Samaritan provides an example of generosity).
- 2 Corinthians 9:6 (when we give generously, God repays us in like manner).

Giving Secretly

An effective steward of God is one who gives without expecting to be canonized for that giving. One of the disciplines of a mature Christian is to receive joy from giving without being publicly recognized for that giving. The Bible tells us that the only One who needs to know what we give is God—and He will know and will respond in an appropriate manner.

Scriptural Perspective

- Matthew 6:1-4 (give with the right motives, not calling attention to yourself for your good deed).

Giving Strategically

We are not to be passive, unintelligent keepers of the King's treasury. We have a responsibility to utilize the wealth entrusted to us in ways that would parallel how God Himself might use those resources if He were investing those resources. This requires that we have a sense of God's priorities, His values and His ways of responding to conditions. He expects us to use these resources in a strategic manner, to facilitate His pleasure and to glorify Him.

Scriptural Perspective

- Deuteronomy 14:28,29 (aliens, orphans and widows should be cared for by people of God, through their generous giving).
- Acts 2:44,45 (give to believers as they have need).
- Acts 4:32—5:11 (contribute to the needs of fellow believers without concern of repayment).

Giving Sacrificially

One could argue that it is impossible for us to give sacrificially because none of what we are giving away is ours to start with! However, the Bible indicates that as we utilize the Lord's resources, we are to at least bear in mind that He looks to us to give sacrificially as we encounter the needs of the saints.

Scriptural Perspective

- Mark 12:41-44 (the poor widow gave two coins).
- 2 Corinthians 8:1-9 (Paul commends the Macedonian churches for their spontaneous, generous giving, in spite of their limited means).

Giving Happily

Achieving joy through giving requires a change of heart regarding the act of giving. If we perceive giving to be a process of losing a share of what is rightfully ours, and which therefore prevents us from getting more of what the world has to offer, we will never find joy through giving. However, if we understand that one of the great blessings from God is to have enough material wealth to be able to share it with others who have need, and to therefore mirror the heart of our loving Father, then we may experience the pleasure of giving. Contributing to the well-being of others is a privilege, not a hardship or a chore.

Scriptural Perspective

- 2 Corinthians 8:10-12 (God blesses those who give with an "eager willingness").
- 2 Corinthians 9:7 (God loves a cheerful giver).

Setting an Example

People learn best by watching what others do. Children watch their parents. Adults watch their neighbors and work associates. Nonbelievers watch Christians to see what difference Christianity makes in their lives. One way we can positively influence the world is by giving generously, sacrificially and without fanfare: allowing the world to see that we understand where our wealth comes from and how to use it in a godly manner. We are not to take our giving cues from the world; instead, the Bible calls us to set the standard of generosity in giving.

Scriptural Perspective

- Acts 2:44-47; 4:32-37 (receive in God's name; give it away generously in His name).
- Acts 5:1-10 (always demonstrate integrity in giving).
- 2 Corinthians 9:1,2 (giving generously may encourage others to do the same).
- 2 Corinthians 9:13 (because of your generosity, others will praise God).

Investing in the Future

Our perspective ought to reflect God's—that is, the long view. When we contribute money to a ministry, we are not simply donating for institutional survival, but for the eternal purposes of God that are carried out by His people on earth. We ought to consider our giving an investment, not a giveaway. The return on that investment may be withheld until we enter God's eternal presence, but we have a responsibility to invest His treasure wisely.

Scriptural Perspective

- Matthew 6:19-21 (invest in the future by giving generously on earth).
- Matthew 25:14-30 (handle God's resources as though they are your own investment; seek the greatest return).
- 2 Corinthians 9:6 (you reap what you sow; therefore, sow bountifully).
- 1 Timothy 6:18,19 (giving generously to those in need builds a treasure in heaven).

> **"I DO NOT BELIEVE WE CAN SETTLE HOW MUCH WE OUGHT TO GIVE. I AM AFRAID THE ONLY SAFE RULE IS TO GIVE MORE THAN WE CAN SPARE."**
> **C. S. LEWIS**

Tithing

Some debate remains in the Church whether tithing is an Old Testament concept that is not applicable to modern life or if it is a fundamental biblical principle for which God's people will be held accountable. Those who reject tithing say that Christ's death and resurrection freed us from the tyranny of

> **"MANY PEOPLE GIVE A TENTH TO THE LORD— A TENTH OF WHAT THEY OUGHT TO GIVE."**
> **ANONYMOUS**

the Law, but that we retain a deep responsibility (and debt) to God. Although we may not have to produce a tithe, we should desire in our hearts to be at least that generous, without any sense of legalistic compulsion. A majority of today's pastors, however, maintain that tithing is still a pertinent concept, one that Jesus Himself supported during His earthly ministry.

Our research has discovered, however, that just one-third of all born-again Christians who attend a church (35 percent) and one-fifth of non-Christians who attend a Christian church (22 percent) believe that the Bible teaches us to tithe. Two out of three adults believe the Bible offers suggestions about giving, but leaves the final choice totally up to us.

Whichever side of the controversy you choose to endorse, the common ground is this: God expects us to be generous givers and to provide a generous share of our firstfruits for His work.

Scriptural Perspective

- Genesis 14:20 (even in plundering an opponent, Abraham gave God 10 percent).
- Leviticus 27:30 (the tithe belongs to the Lord and is holy to Him).
- Deuteronomy 14:22 (always set aside a tenth for God).
- Nehemiah 10:37-39 (Nehemiah commanded all of Israel to give their tenth fastidiously).
- Malachi 3:8-10 (refusal to tithe is robbing God; tithing will cause Him to bless the givers).

**"WE SHOULD TRAVEL LIGHT AND LIVE SIMPLY.
OUR ENEMY IS NOT POSSESSIONS, BUT EXCESS."
JOHN STOTT**

Defeating Materialism and Selfishness

Part of the difficulty many people face is that they have become enslaved to money and possessions. The Scriptures warn of being caught up in "stuff" and encourage us to be sure to focus on what is important (i.e., that which is eternal, heavenly and significant). The Bible provides many stories of people who worked hard, achieved big and emerged desperately poor in spirit. Proper priorities are a key to success; those priorities rely not upon acquisition and achievement, but upon obedience and richness of spirit.

Scriptural Perspective

- Ecclesiastes 5:10 (recognize that wealth is meaningless and unsatisfying).

- Matthew 6:19-34 (be anxious about nothing; seek first God's kingdom).
- Matthew 6:24 (master money by serving God with it).
- Matthew 19:16-24 (if the rich cannot part with their wealth, they are not following Christ).
- Luke 12:16-21 (the rich cannot buy God's favor; recognize material goods for what they are).
- Philippians 4:10-13 (Paul was content in all situations, with whatever he had).
- 1 Timothy 6:6-10 (the love of money is the root of all evil).
- James 5:1-6 (wealth distorts our values and lifestyles).

God's Perspective

Jesus was clear in His perspective on wealth and the use of wealth. In short, He believed that those who give to others actually receive more than do those who are the recipients of such giving. Similarly, Jesus promised His followers that no good deed goes unnoticed. We also read that some day, in heaven, we will receive our repayment for the acts of righteousness performed here.

> **"GOD LOOKS NOT FOR THE QUANTITY OF THE GIFT BUT FOR THE QUALITY OF THE GIVER."**
> **ANONYMOUS**

Scriptural Perspective

- Matthew 10:42 (no act of generosity done in His name will go unseen or unrewarded).
- Acts 20:35 (Jesus said it is more blessed to give than to receive).

God's Response

When people show their full faith in God, He responds. Often we face financial challenges; often those challenges are tests of our will and behavior. God is always looking for an excuse to bless us; when we give Him a reasonable chance, He invariably outblesses us.

Scriptural Perspective

- 2 Kings 4:1-7 (just as the widow who received oil from Elisha was blessed, so God blesses us for being obedient).
- Proverbs 28:27 (giving to the poor brings God's approval).
- Matthew 14:14-21 (when they gave Him what they had, Jesus multiplied five loaves and two fish to feed more than 5,000).
- Matthew 15:32-38 (when they gave Him what they had, Jesus again multiplied it, this time seven loaves and a few fish to feed more than 4,000).
- Philippians aa4:14-17 (when Paul was in need, the Philippians supported him, and they will be credited accordingly).

The Church's Response

Churches have a duty to take people's investment in the ministry seriously. They can demonstrate that attitude by using the gifts provided by donors efficiently and efficaciously to advance the ministry priorities of the congregation. The church is called to provide a balance between satisfying the needs of the church body and those of people outside the church.

Scriptural Perspective

- Acts 6:1-7 (the church should use people's gifts efficiently and effectively).

How to Proceed

Undeniably, the American Church requires a good dose of insight and wisdom regarding stewardship. But how can we deliver the goods to the people who need them? At the risk of seeming simplistic, the apostle Paul's words in 2 Timothy 4:2 emerge as a reasonable strategy: "Preach the Word." God's Word consistently and boldly speaks to the issue of stewardship and what He expects of us. Do not leave the people in your congregation uninformed or misinformed.

chapter

6

Preparing People for Effective Stewardship

"A LOT OF PEOPLE ARE WILLING TO GIVE GOD
THE CREDIT, BUT NOT TOO MANY ARE WILLING
TO GIVE HIM THE CASH."

ANONYMOUS

Acts 8 records the story of the Ethiopian official who had traveled to Jerusalem to worship God. As he was sitting in his carriage, returning to the palace, he was struggling with the Scriptures of Isaiah. He was frustrated because he was reading about things in which he had little training. Fortunately, Philip was exhorted by the Holy Spirit to approach the Ethiopian and assist him in understanding the Scriptures.

In Exodus 18, Moses is going through his daily paces as the dispenser of justice for the Jewish people. At the time, his father-in-law, Jethro, was visiting. A respected leader himself, Jethro accompanied Moses to the court and observed Moses as he attempted to settle disputes among the people. After a day of observing the tension and pressure that had become a daily routine for Moses, Jethro helped his son-in-law conceive and implement a more expeditious justice system, freeing Moses to focus on other leadership issues.

In both of these instances, good people were wrestling with tasks that were overwhelming them. The Ethiopian was unable to fathom the meaning of the prophetic writings because he lacked preparation for the task. Moses was handcuffed by the necessity of mediating community contentions, unable to conceive of a superior means of handling the massive volume of interpersonal divisions.

These were good men, seeking to do what was right, but ill-prepared for the tasks facing them. It took a more learned, better-equipped friend to come alongside and prepare them to meet the daunting challenges they faced. Both Moses and the Ethiopian official were perfectly capable, but wholly unprepared. All it took was some wisdom, insight and practice to enable the two servants of God to rise to the challenge.

Stewardship in the American Church is hindered by a similar lack of preparation among the people. Think about the motivations we discussed in chapter 3. Does your church present a compelling cause? Does it perform its ministry duties effectively? Does it perform its ministry efficiently? Is the church addressing urgent needs? Do people receive personal benefits from your church that make it a ministry worth supporting? Are people able to develop a significant relationship with the church? The answer to all these questions can be a resounding yes!

We know from our discussion in chapter 4 that most adults who attend church services have, at best, a muddled and rudimentary understanding of money and stewardship. Even if their lives depended on it they could not completely and accurately describe God's principles regarding the behavior and responsibilities of a good steward.

In spite of this inability, the adults who attend your church are not bad people (apart from their innately sinful nature). The fact that they attend church, occasionally read the Bible, typically pray to God during the week and believe that their faith is an important component in their lives suggests that they have more than just a passing interest in knowing and serving God. Being largely ignorant of how to do so, however, the typical church attender cannot, except by accident, be a good steward. Just as Moses and the Ethiopian needed assistance, so do most church attenders need someone to help them understand how to be good stewards.

That's where you come in.

Strategic Preparation for Stewardship

Before we can discuss the substance of strategy and tactics for fund-raising and stewardship, we have to consider what it would take to prepare God's people to be good stewards. In this chapter, we will discuss four steps that might be helpful in paving the way for churched adults to comprehend stewardship and become ready to assume their responsibilities as stewards of God's resources.

In the succeeding chapters we will explore companion actions that enable a church to implement a comprehensive, biblical and compelling resource development effort. Those efforts relate to partnership in ministry, audience segmentation, marketing and communications, and leadership. Before we can begin to activate the steps involved in those domains, your congregation must have the proper biblical, emotional and logistical preparation.

> **GOOD STEWARDSHIP DOES NOT JUST HAPPEN. PEOPLE MUST BE STRATEGICALLY PREPARED FOR IT.**

The first step is communicating biblical perspectives and principles to potential donors.

Second, the church must develop a budget for the coming fiscal year.

Third, the congregation must be made aware of the church's financial needs.

Finally, it is important to identify different ways in which people might respond to those needs.

Full Disclosure

Although Americans are comparatively generous people, as measured by the amount and percentage of their income they give away, donating does not come naturally—even for Christians. Thus, a crucial role of the church is to infuse a mental and emotional understanding of the principles, motivations and mechanics of stewardship. Our preaching and teaching should address all matters related to resource acquisition and management. This should include what resources constitute wealth, where our wealth comes from, why we have it, a theological evaluation of resources, how we are to handle them and how God evaluates our performance as His trustees. Naturally, the Bible is our core reference in helping people wrestle with these issues. The magnitude and urgency of the need for stewardship education is profound, as signaled by people's thin base of stewardship knowledge (detailed in the previous chapter).

Some church leaders have been surprised to learn that preaching and teaching about tithing and stewardship is not simply a biblical imperative, but that most churched people appreciate being informed of, and challenged to live up to their personal spiritual calling—when this process is handled with love and sensitivity. As I studied the best fund-raising churches in the nation, it was obvious that the practical, no-holds-barred preaching and teaching of the biblical principles of stewardship, and relentlessly holding the Body of believers accountable to those truths in appropriate ways, were cherished distinctives of these families of Christians devoted to growing even in the difficult, sacrificial aspects of the faith.

Outsiders might expect that pastors and teachers in churches across the country would relish the task of educating the faithful about matters of stewardship. Indeed, by gifting and by training, most pastors describe themselves as teachers or preachers. They tend to be most comfortable when they have opportunities to explicate scriptural texts for open-minded students. I cannot count the number of pastors I have spoken with, in confidence, who have admitted that they struggle with leading, counseling and administrating, but live for chances to study and teach from the Bible.

> **MOST CHURCHED PEOPLE APPRECIATE BIBLICAL TEACHING ABOUT THEIR PERSONAL SPIRITUAL RESPONSIBILITIES—EVEN THOSE RELATED TO GIVING.**

I have also learned from these discussions, as well as from our research, that all Bible teaching does not bring equal degrees of joy and excitement to these gifted communicators. One of the most laudable qualities of most preachers is their topical versatility; most of them are able to challenge the audience, week after week, with helpful insights and thought-provoking questions about subjects ranging from apples (see Garden of Eden) to zithers (as in David's musical instruments). Pastors, however, generally seem to dislike preaching about three foci: topics about which they are completely ignorant, political issues and anything related to financial responsibility.

Nevertheless, 9 out of 10 pastors (87 percent) preach sermons about stewardship and fiscal responsibility during the course of a typical year. Among those who preach about this matter, 4 out of 10 (39 percent) preach a single sermon during the year about giving. One out of three (34 percent) preach two or more sermons about giving as part of a series of that topic. The remaining one-quarter (27 percent) preach two or more sermons about the topic, but do not deliver them consecutively, as part of a money-focused series. In spite of the fear many teachers feel prior to delivering messages about giving and stewardship, their experience indicates that such trepidation is unwarranted. Just one out of every six pastors (16 percent) says he usually receives an abnormally large number of negative reactions from people after delivering such a sermon.

Does it help to teach or preach about stewardship? Consider this pattern of outcomes gleaned from our research.

- Churches in which pastors preach a single message about giving raise more money, per capita, than do those churches in which no preaching about stewardship takes place.
- Churches in which pastors preach two or more nonconsecutive

messages about stewardship responsibilities and practices do not have any fund-raising advantage, per capita, over churches in which just one such sermon is preached during the year.

- Churches in which pastors preach two or more consecutive messages about stewardship topics raise more money, per capita, than do churches that hear a single message about giving. They are also twice as likely to witness increased giving during that year.
- Churches in which pastors preach two or more consecutive messages about stewardship matters raise significantly more money, on a per capita basis, than do churches that hear two or more nonconsecutive money messages.
- Churches in which pastors preach a series of messages about giving are nearly two-and-a-half times more likely to experience an increase in giving than when preachers speak about giving, one sermon at a time, on two or more nonconsecutive occasions during the year.

Clearly, there is a tangible benefit to emphasizing the biblical teachings about money, stewardship and church responsibilities. There is also a benefit to concentrated doses of wisdom about stewardship: Preaching a stewardship series has a much greater and more predictable effect than does preaching unrelated, time-remote stewardship messages throughout the year.

Two common threads that course through the sermons of the effective fund-raisers are the concepts of "lifestyle stewardship" (i.e., treating every resource encountered as another opportunity to serve God by carefully managing that asset) and tithing. Tithing may be controversial to some, and ignored by the masses, but it certainly gets its fair share of promotion from the pulpit. Four out of five pastors who preach about giving speak about the importance of tithing during those messages.

Appropriate Communications
One lesson derived from our research is that people need clear and biblical instructions about their stewardship responsibilities—and they are open to, and grateful for, such teaching. It is equally important, though, that the teaching be credible and accurate. We noted five ways in which it is possible for a well-intentioned teacher to trivialize or compromise the truth of God's stewardship principles. Beware of such teaching; the ends do not justify the means! The following descriptions emphasize these errant approaches of informing people about the privilege and the responsibilities related to stewardship.

Emphasizing clever slogans. The basis of stewardship is Scripture, not cute marketing. We may be able to generate slogans that would make Madison Avenue proud, but make God cringe. Among those you may have encountered are such slogans as, "The more you give, the more you get"; "Give until it hurts"; and "The mark of a committed Christian is giving generously to the church." Other slogans we have heard may be less effective in marketing, but at least they are biblically defensible (e.g., "You can't outgive God").

Proving God's point through proof texts. In our zeal to champion God's perspective, we sometimes take shortcuts in truth. This is most commonly accomplished by taking poignant Bible verses out of context, and building a persuasive argument around "proof texts"—fragments of a larger statement in Scripture that can be conveniently lifted to make the desired case. I encountered instances of preachers using Malachi 3:8-10 as a promise from God that when you give generously to the church, God has obligated Himself to give back to you even more generously. I have heard Bible teachers explain to people that "money is the root of all evil" and they should therefore rid themselves of the "devil's tool." (Of course, the Scripture from which this is taken—1 Timothy 6:10—says the problem is the "love of money.") Be careful that you do not distort God's Word to give greater weight to your own words—even if it is done for laudable, righteous purposes.

Replacing a desire to give with the desire to receive. The success of the "prosperity doctrine" teachers has been well documented. In a self-absorbed, selfish society, the idea of giving so you can get is attractive. The Bible teaches, however, that God looks not only at the act, but also at the motives behind the action. He was displeased with the Pharisees and Sadducees because they were legalistic, following the letter of His Law, but rejecting the spirit that should have been behind their resulting behavior.

Inspiring people to give generously because it forces God to give to us even more generously is a perversion of His Word. Does God indicate that He wishes to bless His people abundantly? Yes. Does He tell us that He will take care of our needs? Yes. Does the Bible teach that we can force God to multiply our investment in His kingdom, a kind of ironclad eternal guarantee that He will return a greater dollar amount to us than we deposit in His work? No.

Forsaking true ministry for productive methodology. Sometimes we become focused on techniques rather than on the purposes for which we employ those techniques. Keep in mind that the best way to mature people in stewardship is not by manipulating them through methods, techniques, strategies and plans. The foundation of a true stewardship campaign is ministry. Our primary objective must be to minister in God's truth to the whole person. That means serving them, teaching them, inspiring them, encouraging them, modeling righteousness for them and exhorting them. It does not mean manipulating them through marketing and through emotional pressure.

Have you experienced a church that gives people prizes or premiums according to the size of their gifts? Or churches that enter the name of pledge givers in a special drawing to receive a vacation or object of desire? How about appeals that place the blame on God for the need: "Our church has been so blessed by God that unless you give more generously than ever, we will not be able to maintain the size and breadth of this outreach"? Have you heard appeals that manipulate your emotions: "If you do not give 15 percent more than you gave last year, we will have to eliminate or reduce many of our finest programs—and that certainly can't be God's will for us as a church"?

Keep your eyes focused on the reason for which we raise money: to enable people to be in right relationship with God, and to facilitate effective biblical ministry to God's people. These are ministry purposes, not business purposes. Methods are necessary ways of organizing our behavior and facilitating desirable outcomes, but they must not replace the bottom-line purpose of a stewardship effort: engagement in ministry.

Raising money through emotional pleading. We know that we can raise money by impressing people with an urgent need. We know that people are more likely to give generously when they are exposed to the intense suffering of others. However, we must address some ethical considerations. When we present such images and circumstances to donors, are we providing a valid representation of circumstances and how the money they donate will be used? Is the use of gripping graphics and heart-wrenching stories merely a fund-raising ploy designed to manipulate people's emotions? Do we imply that if we have sufficient funding we will eliminate the shocking conditions we have portrayed? Are the testimonies of changed lives we parade in front of the congregation a legitimate reflection of the nature, quality and focus of our ministry efforts and outcomes?

To maintain credibility for the cause of Christ and for your church, avoid excessively dramatic or misleading fund-raising appeals that tug at people's heartstrings. It is ethically permissible to move people emotionally, but we must do so in conjunction with our responsibility as communicators of truth to provide people with a balanced presentation of the realities we seek to address through the funds raised.

The Vocal Minority

Financial support for churches remains a controversial concern to many people. Surprisingly few people have strong intellectual convictions about how churches teach about, raise and use money. For many, it is a major emotional issue. The comments we heard reflected the breadth of misunderstanding and dissatisfaction among many people regarding church fund-raising practices and theology. Among the comments collected from the laity were:

"Churches care more about money than about people."

"Churches spend too much time talking about money—my money."

"Churches need to be run more like businesses, more efficiently."

"Why do churches need so much money if most of the work is done by volunteers?"

"If all money is God's, why does the church constantly have to beg for more of it?"

We need to put the anecdotal evidence aside, though, and consider the magnitude of people's feelings about churches and money to gain a more objective viewpoint. In spite of some vocal concerns about the monetary side of ministry, we also discovered that most church people are satisfied with how their church handles the money it receives. They may not have a deep understanding of what happens to their money once it is given to the church, but they are generally confident that it is used for acceptable purposes.

Even more interesting was the revelation that people are not only open to learning more about their personal stewardship responsibilities, but many would also take part in the fund-raising activities of the church if they were asked to help and offered a role they could handle well. Interestingly, it seems that the larger the church, the more likely the laity are to desire a role in the fund-raising procedures.

Conventional wisdom suggests that people want nothing to do with fund-raising—and ample *anecdotal* evidence supports such thinking. *Empirical* evidence, however, demonstrates that a sufficiently large cadre of laity are interested in helping to raise money for ministry. This suggests that pastors serving churches of more than 100 people should not feel anxious about, or alone in, the effort to bring in money for ministry.

Defeating Failure

Not surprisingly, we were informed by a sizable minority of pastors who preach about giving and stewardship that they see no increase or change in giving habits resulting from their preaching. This has become a source of tremendous frustration and embarrassment to most of these preachers.

Why, then, do many pastors who notice no upturn in giving after such sermons continue to preach about the topic, year after year? These pastors mentioned various reasons. Some continue to hope that people will finally catch the message and respond. Others contend that to effectively shepherd the people they must continually expose the flock to teaching that stretches and challenges them, regardless of their responses.

Another perspective emerged: Some pastors refuse to judge the value or appropriateness of their sermons according to perceptible outcomes in people's lives or in developing the church. For all these leaders, then, sermons will continue to be preached about giving, no matter what happens in response to such messages.

Budgeting for Dollars

Biblical teaching about financial responsibility and opportunities is one step toward preparing people to be great stewards for God. It takes more than just information, however, to persuade people to practice good stewardship.

As any good business leader will note, one of the most important steps in building a successful enterprise is intelligent, accurate budgeting. Having spent more than a decade as a consultant working with major corporations—from Disney to Prudential—I have seen firsthand how seriously the "major players" take their budgets.

There is good news on the budgeting front: The vast majority of churches have an annual budget. The quality and utility of those documents, however, varies greatly. The limited significance attached to budgets in tens of thousands of Protestant churches relates to the widely held perception among pastors and church staffs that a church is a ministry, not a business. The implications of this perception are compounded by the fact that few churches have pastors or staff who are experienced or well educated in basic business practices. Churches are most strikingly distinguishable from for-profit organizations in relation to how they handle finances—and budgeting is a prime example of the uniqueness of churches.

We discerned three dominant approaches among churches in planning their finances. About half of all churches approach fund-raising by first developing a budget for the upcoming year, then seeking to raise the funding to meet the proposed budget. One-third of all Protestant churches reverse that process: They initially estimate how much money they believe they will be able to raise during the year and then develop a budget accordingly. The remaining churches have a variety of hybrid strategies they follow to reconcile ministry and money.

> **A GOOD BUDGET IS A NECESSARY INGREDIENT IN AN EFFECTIVE MIX OF STEWARDSHIP ACTIVITIES.**

The purpose of this book is not to explain the mechanics of budgeting. It is important to recognize, however, that the quality of the budget developed by a church intimately affects the church's ability to raise money for ministry.

First, it raises people's consciousness about the level of finances it will take to enable the church to minister in line with its mission.

Second, it solidifies the church's ministry priorities.

Third, creating a budget says something about the foresight and sophistication of the church's leaders.

Fourth, budgets send a message to people in the church about the level of generosity they must exhibit if the church is going to satisfy its ministry obligations.

The church budget is a strategic tool in preparing people for effective personal stewardship. The seriousness with which church leaders take the budget will be reflected in the seriousness with which donors take their responsibility to fund the ministry. Be careful not to treat your church budget, and the related process of developing that budget, as just another must-do activity. Such an attitude will diminish people's interest in making the budget come to life.

Acute Awareness

Budgets can help people understand the goals and priorities of the ministry. It will take more than developing a budget, though, to adequately inform the entire congregation of what the church needs the money for and how much money people will need to give to make the ministry efforts successful.

Unless the church can realistically provide people with a sense of the significance and the urgency of the financial need, the people will merely yawn and look to other, more needy organizations. Even the most affluent churches are able to describe their ministry plans and adventures in terms of the necessity of raising specific sums of money to reach people-related goals, the significance of irretractable commitments and the importance of timing in raising ministry funds.

Churches that effectively raise money to get the job done invariably proclaim that it is not simply enough to present a detailed plan for activity—the people in the pews are exposed to plans and schedules all the time. To motivate people to take their responsibility as stewards seriously, the church must work hard to sell people on the spiritual influence of the ministry endeavors being promoted. The experience of these churches has shown that unless potential donors grasp the possible effect of the proposed ministry and harbor a clear sense of the urgency of the need, the chances of their donating generously are limited.

> **PEOPLE WILL NOT GIVE TO MEET NEEDS THEY DO NOT KNOW EXIST.**

The Bible makes no bones about the fact that we often do not get what we want because we do not ask for it specifically, and that sometimes when we ask specifically we ask for the wrong reasons (see Jas. 4:2,3). Usually, the stumbling block is not that churches are asking for the wrong reasons; in my observations, it is extremely rare to find a church that has inappropriate motives. The downfall is that most churches simply do not ask people intensely and precisely enough to stimulate them to give. As professional fund-raisers will assert, "the ask" must be clear, compelling, believable, well-thought through and specific. The manner in which the need is presented often influences a person's determination of whether or not to give, and it certainly influences the amount of money they choose to donate.

Presenting the need for funding is a vital component in preparing people for effective stewardship. A weak response from the congregation may reflect more about how the need is presented than about the willingness of the congregation to support effective and significant ministry efforts.

Laying Out the Options

Once people are aware of the church's needs and feel comfortable giving to meet those needs, they need to know the alternative ways they can provide financial support.

Churches have tried a wide range of activities to raise the money needed for ministry. For all the experimentation that occurs, though, only a limited degree of creativity or risk is taken by most churches in fund-raising. Most churches rely upon just a handful of common tactics—approaches such as asking people to tithe, taking free-will offerings, instituting a pledge system to anticipate giving levels or perhaps utilizing a stewardship campaign.

Different dynamics are at work in small and large churches. Congregations that operate on less than $100,000 annually are much more likely to rely upon free-will offerings, almost exclusively, than to develop some kind of holistic fund-development strategy that is set forth in the course of weeks or months. Deficits or shortfalls are commonly covered through bake sales, rummage sales and other kinds of small events put together by members of the congregation.

Large churches, on the other hand, generally create a more broad-based fund-raising program. A common component in the program is one or more special weekend services or sermons addressing the responsibility of believers to donate to the work of the ministry.

My assessment of what works best for churches is that it is important to treat church finances as a significant element in ministry, and that this is best accomplished by having a stewardship campaign.

The Stewardship Campaign

The notion of a "stewardship campaign" has a multitude of connotations to church leaders. Such a campaign is effective when it integrates pertinent needs, opportunities and resources into a mix that facilitates the ministry God designed for the church.

In practice, stewardship campaigns encompass a wide range of elements. The single element most commonly included in campaigns is teaching provided to the entire Body (usually in the context of worship services) about biblical standards for giving. Most churches that conduct stewardship campaigns also include communications that provide a detailed understanding of the church's financial condition and descriptions of the specific needs of the ministry. In most cases, this constitutes verbal communication to a group of people gathered specifically for this purpose (either in a church service or at a special meeting).

Roughly one out of three churches that implements a campaign conveys the financial goals of the church to the people through mailed communications. About half of the campaign churches sponsor face-to-face meetings with people (sometimes one-on-one meetings, usually group meetings) in which church participants are encouraged to give generously to the church in consideration of the identified needs. A majority of the churches engaged in stewardship campaigns also incorporated pledge systems in their efforts. A smaller proportion included all-church meals or other special events to inform people of the church's needs and to solicit their support.

Pledging Gifts

Another popular approach in raising money is to ask people to make a voluntary, nonbinding pledge to indicate the amount of money they expect to donate to the church within a specified period of time. These pledges are generally defined for the prospective donors as a "soft" commitment—a sum the donor plans to give but may change during the pledge period. In other words, pledges are flexible commitments made in good faith. Overall, 4 out of every 10 Protestant churches make pledging a regular part of their fund-raising efforts.

> **WHEN MANAGED DEFTLY, PLEDGING BECOMES A WIN-WIN STRATEGY FOR CHURCHES AND THEIR SUPPORTERS.**

The pastors of pledge-based churches typically endorse the process as helpful to everyone involved. For the donors, the pledge process requires them to think and pray about their financial responsibilities to their church. The pledge itself represents an act of faith and a tangible barometer against which God's provision and their own faithfulness can be measured. For the church's leaders, the pledges become a reasonable estimate of a percentage of the church's giving. That base enables the leaders to plan more effectively and adjust the ministry budget as necessary. Such planning removes much of the natural anxiety and guesswork from developing ministry operations.

Pastors of these churches estimate that about 60 percent of the congregation, on average, participate in the pledge process. Pledging is not simply an exercise in wishful thinking, either. These pastors note that the vast majority of people who turn in a pledge make good on it. For three-quarters of the churches that use a pledge system, more than 80 percent of their people fulfill their entire pledge. Only 1 out of every 10 churches claims that less than 70 percent of their body deliver what they had hoped to provide.

Pledge income is vitally important for most of the churches that use the pledge system. On average, more than two-thirds of the church's aggregate revenue base is from those people who gave a pledge to the church. Most churches that engage in pledging seek to assist people in fulfilling their commitments by sending them updated statements during the year. This informs donors of how much they have given to fulfill their pledges.

The churches that have found pledges to be most useful and productive are those that rely upon a team of laypeople to oversee the fund-raising activities of the church. Those churches are twice as likely to incorporate pledging in their stewardship mix as are churches that rely primarily upon the pastor or church staff to oversee raising money.

Fund-Raising Events

A surprisingly small proportion of churches plan events geared to raising money for the ministry (40 percent). Large churches are more likely to sponsor fund-raising events than are small churches—largely because events are too labor intensive for a small church to handle.

Among the churches that use events to raise funds, an average of three events are sponsored per year. The main reasons comparatively few churches utilize events is that they are labor intensive and they add relatively little to the church coffers. The rare church is able to raise even 10 percent of its budget through its schedule of events.

Ninety-two percent of the pastors surveyed concluded that their events have been successful. Many indicated, however, that although the events were ostensibly planned to raise funds, they proved to be more productive in building relationships among congregants, enhancing ownership of the church's vision and developing better teamwork among church leaders. Interestingly, I also found that most pastors have rather low expectations of events. Many deem these events successful if they simply raise, rather than lose, money, no matter what the positive cash flow amount might be.

Churches sponsor myriad events designed to raise money. The most common of those events are the following:

- Meals (dinners, breakfasts, banquets)   63 percent
- Sales (rummage, bake, bazaars, crafts)   55 percent
- Entertainment (concerts, theater, talent)   15 percent
- Car washes   8 percent
- Carnivals, fairs, circus   7 percent

Perhaps another reason for the limited enthusiasm regarding fund-raisers as a source of revenue is that the revenue to be produced is both unpredictable and hard to collect. For instance, most churches rely upon free-will offerings at the entertainment events and meals. It is virtually impossible to accurately anticipate the income that will be generated at sales or other service activities (e.g., car washes). Churches are often bashful about asking the people attending the event to contribute money. Six out of 10 churches that use events for fund-raising say they never ask the people at these events for money: People give on an "as-led" basis.

Planned Giving

A surprisingly large proportion of churches claim to receive revenues from the estates of deceased members. Overall, 4 out of every 10 churches receive some kind of income in a typical year from legacies.

The research showed that large churches are more likely to receive planned gifts than are small churches. Although 39 percent of the churches that have small budgets received such wealth transfers, 59 percent of the largest churches were the beneficiaries of such giving. Among the reasons for this difference is the fact that churches that have large budgets are more intentional and aggressive in encouraging people to name the church as a beneficiary of their estates.

Among the churches that have budgets of less than $100,000, barely one-third actively pursue such donations; among the large churches, more than half (53 percent) invite people to do so. Another key reason for the greater success of large churches in legacy giving is that they have more people to draw from when they are recruiting such givers.

More About Stewardship Campaigns

Based on my research, I am a big supporter of handling fund-raising and stewardship in a campaign context. Every great stewardship campaign I have studied was shaped to the unique characteristics of the church. Yet I also found that great campaigns have several elements in common. The ever-present components include the following:

- Strong lay leadership of the campaign. Putting the pastor in charge of the campaign will limit the effectiveness of both the pastor and the campaign (more about this in chapter 9).
- The campaign must be run professionally and efficiently.
- The campaign should unfold over a period of at least one month, not including a period of prior, public anticipation of its coming.
- The campaign is consistently related to funding goals that have been adequately described and justified to the congregation.

Many of those goals are embedded within the budget, which serves as a foundational document for the campaign.

- A series of messages regarding the biblical concept of steward-ship is integrated into the mix of activities.
- Regular updates about the status of the campaign are provided to the congregants. (Incidentally, "giving thermometers"—the large thermometers used to graphically depict the level of support promised, shown by the mercury level inside the thermometer—are widely frowned upon as a means of conveying pledged amounts, if pledging is used.)
- Reference is made to the process as a stewardship campaign, not as a fund-raising campaign.
- The campaign is an annual process.

Stewardship campaigns are not a panacea, but they appear to provide the best structure for strategies designed to raise stewardship consciousness. They create the desired atmosphere for learning and reflecting about giving and for delivering on the financial needs of the church.

Choosing a Great Campaign Manager
Upon graduating from college, one of my first jobs was managing campaigns for candidates running for public office. I learned a lot of important lessons for life from those high-pressure, exhausting campaigns. One of the lessons was this: A great candidate will lose the election if he or she has a mediocre campaign manager.

The same is true of stewardship campaigns at churches. The church's ministry might be superb, but if the campaign is not well managed, the church will suffer financially. Assuming that the pastor is not the primary director of the campaign—and he should not be—then how do you identify someone who would be a great campaign director?

It would be worth your time to develop a checklist of criteria to define a great stewardship campaign director. To help in your thinking about the most helpful criteria, the following are some of my observations of the qualities and abilities of the volunteers who have done a superb job in the director role.

- *Moderate to high profile within the congregation.* The professionalism and credibility of your campaign is aided immensely by having a known, liked and respected person take the reigns of the campaign. A person who has such a profile commands the attention of others more easily and provides an extra level of comfort to potential donors.
- *High level of personal integrity and credibility.* It takes more than having a person who is well known and liked. The person is

handling a sensitive topic—money—and must therefore be highly trusted by the people. If the campaign chairperson does not inspire confidence, neither will he or she inspire generosity.

- *Consistent church attendance.* It will be difficult to persuade regular attenders—who happen to be the most consistent and most generous givers, in most cases—to take the campaign seriously if someone who does not appear to be fully invested in the ministry leads the stewardship effort. The leader should be "one of their own"—someone they know has a commitment to the church that is equal to, if not greater than, their own. When an irregular attender is chosen as the chairperson, the campaign smacks of sterile professionalism: Responsibility has been placed in the hands of someone who may have the appropriate knowledge and skills, but not the same heartbeat for the ministry.

- *Well informed about the many dimensions of the church's endeavors.* As the chief spokesperson for the financial needs of the church, the campaign director must be thoroughly versed and conversant in the ministries and related financial needs of the church. Naturally, no layperson will have encyclopedic knowledge of these matters, but being sufficiently versed to speak authoritatively and to make decisions with confidence, as well as having a commitment to provide the answers people want, are keys to being effective in this position.

- *Good public speaker.* One of the unavoidable jobs of the stewardship leader is speaking to the congregation and subgroups within it in public settings. This requires the chairperson to be not only sincere, but also a proficient public speaker. A good campaign director is an effective salesperson—not in the sense of manipulating people, but in terms of understanding and addressing their needs as potential supporters.

- *Capable of enlisting and motivating people, and delegating tasks.* Running a great campaign transcends the abilities of even the most capable and experienced person. Great stewardship campaigns require strong teams to share the burden. The best campaign directors are true leaders: they surround themselves with capable people who understand the vision, accept responsibility, have complementary gifts and skills, and take direction from the leader while working independently. A great leader not only identifies and recruits such people, but also encourages them along the way and monitors their progress to keep the program on track.

- *Good with deadlines.* Every campaign has a finite calendar. Creating and sticking to plans that fit within that window of focus are important. A director who misses deadlines is a director who loses opportunities and squanders people's efforts.

- *Able and willing to commit a lot of time.* Do not attempt to minimize the time commitment an effective campaign consumes when recruiting a director. Anything done right takes time. If a qualified person is the first choice, but is too busy to allocate much time to the effort—and this is not unusual because the most qualified people are usually the busiest—try to accommodate both parties, but do not shortchange the campaign. In the event that the primary candidate simply cannot devote the necessary time to the effort, consider a cochair situation, dividing the responsibilities between two excellent but busy people.

- *Does not need another position to build personal prestige.* If someone wants the position because it will be a stepping stone to bigger and better things, the person is wrong for the job. Just as it is necessary to determine and address the motivations of donors, so it is important to be wary of the motivations of those who are willing to direct the stewardship campaign. It is reasonable for someone to view effectively managing the campaign as a means of proving leadership and commitment to the church; after all, there have to be some intangible rewards to those who accept this difficult task. Be careful, though, of people who lack a servant's attitude. Their focus must be doing what is good for the church, not simply what elevates them to prominence.

- *A great team player.* Campaigns are team efforts. The leader may have the highest profile, but the entire team must be encouraged, appreciated and supported. The director is the captain of a team, not a one-person show and a supporting cast. Does your candidate have good team-building skills?

- *Willing to take direction from the pastor and elders.* The director is under the leadership of the senior pastor and the elders of the church. This relationship needs to be clear from the outset. The senior pastor and elders, however, must also respect the campaign director enough to provide him or her with the freedom to make decisions without gaining approval each time. It may be wise to outline the kinds of decisions, if any, that will require the input of the pastor or elders. This should be an accountability relationship, but not a suffocating relationship.

- *In good health.* It helps if the director is in good health. This job takes stamina and energy; it is wise to avoid individuals whose frail health might limit their ability to meet deadlines, interact with people or invest time in necessary procedures.

- *Creative problem solver.* Like any leadership post, this one will demand that problems be solved. Generally, avoid recruiting someone who is incapable of intelligently handling problems that arise, or one who is so timid that every conundrum is brought to the pastor's attention. Every campaign raises more than just money: problems are invariably raised, too. Do you know of someone who not only has the creative thinking and strong communication skills to facilitate problem solving, but also the guts to make tough calls and the sound judgment to win your trust?

Now that is an impressive list of attributes. After I initially constructed the list, I realized that if I could find such a person, I should immediately hire him or her for my company—probably to replace me! The chances are better than even that you will not find a person in your congregation who meets every one of these criteria, so you may be looking for the most capable candidate, not the perfect director.

Keep in mind that each of these criteria are not of equal value. For instance, you could argue that finding someone who has high levels of personal integrity and credibility is more important than selecting someone who is well informed about all the aspects of the church's ministry. Both qualifications are important. However, you can educate a great candidate about the details of the church's ministry; but you cannot quickly teach someone about ethics and morality and make him or her into a person of integrity, because that quality must be proven with time and experience.

As you consider what you are looking for in a campaign director, prioritize the qualities you are seeking so that each candidate is evaluated according to the most important of the qualities you desire.

The notion of a hierarchy of important qualities is supported by a study done a few years ago by one of the nation's fund-raising experts. Jerold Panas tried to identify the most important qualities required to become a successful fund-raiser. Initially, his research resulted in 88 qualities, which were then narrowed to the 30 most important. Still concerned that such a shopping list of characteristics was too extensive, he conducted further research that resulted in 10 indispensable traits, listed in descending order of importance.

1. impeccable integrity
2. a good listener
3. ability to motivate
4. high energy
5. concern for people
6. high expectations
7. love fund-raising
8. have perseverance
9. presence
10. quality of leadership[1]

Notice that Panas's list is different from mine, and probably different from yours. In your context, the only list that matters is yours.

The moral of this story is not to disqualify someone who does not meet all your criteria, because no perfect person exists, and some criteria are more critical than others. The best strategy is to know what you are looking for, seek the most qualified person and invite that person to champion the campaign.

The Secret to Success

I have no quantitative data to back up my final point about stewardship campaigns, but I believe it is accurate. More importantly, I believe it is truly the secret to running a successful campaign. The secret is this: The campaign should be completed before you officially begin it.

Now this may sound like impossible, contradictory nonsense. What it means, though, is that if you have to wait until the four weeks of your campaign to instill within people a passion for the church, an understanding of the vision, an ownership of the ministry and a sense of responsibility to help, then it is too late to win people over. I have no doubt that a sterling four-week campaign will increase people's generosity, and it may build a degree of commitment and ministry understanding that did not previously exist, and would not have emerged otherwise. Such gains, however, are incremental; they are a quick fix, in danger of dissipating once the next sermon series starts.

At the great fund-raising churches in America, stewardship is a perpetual theme, not a special campaign. The ongoing ministry efforts at those churches do not separate stewardship from other ministry endeavors, but integrate stewardship thinking and behavior into every ministry practice and program. One of the pastors of a church that is a stewardship model described his church's approach in such terms:

> We are relentlessly seeking participatory ministry, helping people to grow, and identifying opportunities for them to help others grow. My job is not to preach, but to encourage and equip. My staff's jobs are not singles ministry, Christian education, worship and so forth; they all have the same job, and that is to encourage and equip people. If we knock ourselves out nurturing the saints, that model engenders an inevitable question: What can I do to help? What can I do to return something to these [ministry staff] people who have been so supportive, so helpful, so loving? Our response is to challenge them to be good stewards of all of their resources: their time, their energy, their talents and abilities, their contacts, their money. By the time our annual campaign rolls around, its success depends upon how well we have ministered to the people, not how persuasively I preach about financial responsibilities.

This concept was evident in most of the great fund-raising churches I visited or researched. The campaign is the equivalent of the 100-meter race at the Olympics. The winner is not determined by who participates on the day of the race, but by the hard work and quality of preparation that preceded that day. The athletes that toe the starting line for the race ultimately reap what they have sown in the prior years of practice and personal development. Similarly, if your church waits until Stewardship Month to jar people into remembering that they have a financial obligation to God, you will not run the good race.

Different Strokes
Every church needs to develop its own unique and integrated stewardship strategy. Arriving at a viable strategy requires a lot of experimentation. Most pastors admit that some of their fund-raising efforts have proven ineffective. One of the keys to developing a workable strategy, then, is to test, evaluate, refine and perfect various elements.

Naturally, what works in some churches does not work in others. Effective fund-raising within a church, just like every other ministry, must be tailored to the idiosyncrasies of the people and their context. Sometimes a "proven strategy" does not live up to expectations because of differences in management style or performance quality. Often an approach fails because the stewardship leaders misread the congregation and instigate an approach inappropriate to the nature of the campaign or congregation.

Many other explanations also emerged regarding differences in productivity: the timing of the endeavor, people's sense of ownership of the vision for the ministry and how well the fund-raising efforts coincide with that vision, the perceived intensity of pastoral involvement and the definition of "effective." The key is to not give up trying simply because efforts counted upon did not work.

Note
1. Jerold Panas, *Born to Raise* (Chicago: Pluribus Press, 1988), pp. 212-213.

7

Partnership Strategies

**"ABOUT ALL SOME PEOPLE ARE GIVING
THESE DAYS IS ADVICE."**
ANONYMOUS

One of the hallmarks of today's culture is that people do not want to be passive order takers; they want to be active participants, playing a significant role in the decision making that will determine how they spend their time and energy. This has been taken a step farther by the buster generation, which generally rejects the imposition of any rules, limitations or requirements. In our diverse, decentralized, pluralistic, relativistic society, people expect to be partners.

This mind-set has invaded the stewardship domain as well. Adults are not likely to be content being given the church's goals for the coming year, reading the financial expectations emanating from those goals and receiving a "suggested donation" statement. These days the typical churched adult wants respect, access and input. Potential donors see themselves as vested partners in the ministry and expect to be treated as such.

Perceiving oneself to be a partner and behaving as a full partner in ministry are two different matters, though. What can you do to empower the people in your church to truly become fully invested in the ministry, and to reflect that relationship through their stewardship? Let me continue to describe what our research revealed about effective stewardship, focusing in this chapter on how churches can develop donors as ministry partners.

Casting and Funding Vision

Solomon once wrote, "Where there is no vision, the people perish" (Prov. 29:18, *KJV*). To apply that idea to today's ministry and stewardship efforts, we might state that "without a vision for ministry, the people will devote their resources to nonministry ventures."

People gravitate to a compelling vision of tomorrow. One reason many churches struggle to raise money is that their leaders fail to effectively cast vision for the future. Robert Schuller of the Crystal Cathedral in Garden Grove, planted his church in Southern California and guided it from zero to huge. He then became the most-watched television preacher in America. He conceived the glass cathedral in which his church worships. During the course of his four-decade ministry, he has raised more than $500 million. The secret? "In order to raise money, you have to have a bold vision. It has to be dramatic and exciting. No one has a money problem—only an idea problem."[1]

The vision represents God's big idea for the ministry, the strategic guidance that gives people's lives and ministry meaning. God's vision is the cornerstone of every effective ministry. Without the vision in place, we fall back on whatever comes naturally. Usually, that means we follow the paths of least resistance; those well-worn avenues are rarely the routes to maximum ministry influence.

Given the fact that God's vision is provided to His leaders for building His church and for perfecting His people, the basic elements required for effective vision casting are readily available and accessible. Experience shows that church leaders who effectively promote God's vision are more likely to raise substantial amounts of money to pursue that vision.

> **VISION CONVERTS THE RELUCTANT DONOR
> INTO A RELIABLE DONOR.**

The vision that is articulated for the church must be the vision of God, not that of the pastor. Some of the sustaining qualities of such vision is that it is realistic, widely beneficial, comprehensible and credible. Such vision is based on accepting God's absolute moral and spiritual truths, described in the Bible, which then become the central foundation on which the church's efforts are based. The vision becomes the unique blueprint that will transform society and individuals. For a fund-raising effort to be built upon any other base is a recipe for disaster.[2]

Vision motivates people to action. The people who develop an unwavering sense of commitment to a ministry are most often those who have been exposed to God's vision for the ministry of the church. When the church's leaders are vision driven, they minister with an unusually high degree of spiritual depth and strength of conviction. Such focus and intensity is attractive to most donors.

The importance of enabling the congregation to know and embrace the vision, however, transcends acquiescence to a corporate focus. Enabling potential donors to own the vision as a personal directive from God will deeply influence their felt need to fund the work of their church. Once the vision ceases to belong to the church and instead becomes a part of a person's personal life and ministry, the typical donor becomes aware of the higher purpose to his or her generosity.

Creating Acceptable Goals

Donors must be put in touch with specific, tangible ministry goals that get them excited. One of the objectives of developing and communicating the goals of the ministry to the congregation is to enable people to join into a true partnership with the church.

Those goals must cover a variety of activities, showing people the breadth and depth of the church's ministry. This does not mean that people donate only to megaministries that offer a full slate of programs and activities, or that small churches have no chance for numerical or financial growth. It does mean that part of your task as a resource developer is to enable people to understand what you are asking them to invest in and to provide them with as comprehensive a portrait of your ministry landscape as possible.

In describing ministry goals that require people's financial support, you must advance a convincing case, showing that your ministry is so valuable that donors will lose out on a wonderful opportunity to honor God and serve people if they choose not to become full financial partners in the ministry. Because most church donors and potential donors are aware of other appealing giving opportunities through competing charities, you have to present a case that gives your church a competitive edge.

The magnitude of that challenge is expanded by the reality that people do not get excited about each of the components of your ministry. Some folks get turned on by missions, some by evangelism, some by the beauty or functionality of the campus, some by the counseling that helps people get their lives together. In raising money for the church, we have found that what excites the pastor may not stir the hearts of the congregation. This may come as a shock to either the pastor or people within the church, but absorbing this truth is a healthy behavior. Recognizing the existence of a divergence of enthusiasm may facilitate a broadening of the church's ministry to allow the vision to be pursued from different angles, by different people, all having the same purpose and focus in mind.

Modular Giving

If the adults in your church are turned on by different aspects of the church's ministry, such knowledge should reshape your fund-raising and stewardship endeavors. The key to exploiting this insight is to creatively segment your fund-raising efforts into *ministry modules* and then encourage people to "buy" into one or more of those modules. (A ministry module is an area of ministry characterized by the performance of a particular activity or focus upon a specific people group.)

Many ministry modules need funding. Some modules address ministry to groups of people within the congregation: children, high schoolers, men, women, elderly and so on. Some ministry modules focus on the needs of people outside of the congregation: the homeless, unwed mothers, single moms and AIDS patients. Missions activities provide yet another series of modules: individual missionaries, overseas projects and partnerships with missions organizations. Church programs or ministries that focus primarily on ministering to the donor may also be attractive to donors, enabling people to give to favorite aspects of the church's inreach, such as the music department or the Christian education effort.

The list of ministry modules is virtually endless. The idea underlying modular fund-raising, though, is that people become enthusiastic about giving when the needs and potential influence are narrowed to those areas that excite the donor. In this age of decentralization and specialization, relatively few people get turned on by throwing their comparatively limited donations into a giant ministry money pot.

> **MODULAR GIVING UNLEASHES PEOPLE'S GENEROSITY BY FOCUSING ON THE MINISTRIES THEY CARE MOST DEEPLY ABOUT, WITHOUT RESTRICTING THE USE OF THEIR GIFTS FOR SPECIFIC MINISTRY EFFORTS.**

Because donors are most often stimulated to action by resonance with a cause, influence, efficiency and urgent need, simply placing cash or checks in an offering basket for the upkeep and general work of the church may seem depersonalized, impersonal and void of meaning. When a donor gives with the expectation of playing a significant role in supporting a specific ministry of personal appeal, though, frequently arouses even the least excitable of church supporters. This approach often eliminates the donor's concerns about focus and value, and protects the church's freedom to use funds as necessary to accomplish all aspects of the church's vision.

In its simplest form, here is how modular fund-raising works. Start with a group of people who are part of the stewardship team. That team will sit down with, or call, people in the congregation to speak with them in a nonthreatening, low-pressure manner about the church and its stewardship process. Each of these stewardship associates is responsible for setting up and following through on the visits with each of the adults to whom they have been assigned.

During the visit, the stewardship representative explains the proposed fiscal budget and how the money will be divided among the various core ministries (i.e., ministry modules) of the church. The rep then gathers feedback from the potential donor regarding which ministries, programs or other ministry endeavors are most captivating or inspiring to the donor. The rep then speaks more specifically about the modules identified as being of greatest interest to the donor, emphasizing the influence the person could have by giving generously to the church to facilitate such a ministry effort.

This process is no simple task, of course, because it requires the church to "push the hot buttons" of each donor individually. It takes time and effort to interact with everyone in the church to discern what kinds of ministry turn them on. The results of this effort far outweigh the costs, though.

Using this approach has many advantages. Instead of people giving to the church because of guilt or through the persuasion mustered by force of personality (usually that of the pastor), people give because they feel as though they are giving to *their* church and *their* ministry for outcomes they personally care about and in which they have chosen to invest. We found that donors involved in the modular approach often believe that failing to support their church would harm the health of the church as well as hinder their personal ability to do good works for Christ. Modular giving, in other words, facilitates a tangible sense of ministry ownership in ways that may never be accomplished through more generic, general-fund appeals.

One of the most commonly mentioned benefits of modular fund-raising is that potential donors are less likely to believe the level of funding needed by the church is unreachable or overwhelming. For instance, instead of being asked to donate as much as they can afford to enable the church to reach its $300,000 need, the potential donor may look at a $20,000 Christian education budget, a $17,000 music budget, a $24,000 evangelism budget and so forth. The modularization or segmenting of ministry activities and their associated financial needs makes the aggregate goal seem more bite-sized and achievable than monolithic and beyond their means.

Modular fund-raising also provides donors with the benefit of knowing more about the different aspects of the ministry. This, in turn, tends to enhance their pride in their church and reinforce the belief that God's work is truly being done. Modular marketing of the ministry provides donors with the ability to make choices, which satisfies the typical person's need for control and self-determination. Unless people feel as if the decision of what and how to give is their own, the chances of their providing significant contributions are limited.

Modular giving is not synonymous with designated giving. Effective modular fund-raising disallows designated gifts. Instead, the objective of this strategy is to enable people to see the entire fabric of the ministry and to know that when their money is donated, it is helping to make their favorite ministry activities come alive within the framework of a holistic ministry.

A Common Concern

In presenting the modular concept to pastors, some have expressed the belief that their church could not employ the approach because their church has too many people to permit personal contact with them all. What an odd response for a church!

Having personal contact and gathering input from all potential donors is just one kind of individual interaction the church should have with its people. If the church is truly a community, and if it wishes to understand and be responsive to the needs of the congregation, how can that be fulfilled without constant, planned, strategic interaction with the congregation?

There is no denying that marshaling the people to make consistent contact with the congregation is not a simple task. However, consider this possibility: If your church is "too big" to establish one or more personal contacts with each congregant every year, then your church may simply be "too big" to minister effectively. Size should be viewed as a means to opportunity, not an excuse for impersonal programs.

Addressing the Competition for Ministry Dollars

One of the frequent concerns raised in church circles is that money that would otherwise be given to the local church is diverted to parachurch ministries. Although many parachurch leaders downplay such concern, one of our nationwide surveys of donors revealed that there is some justification for anxiety. One out of seven adults (14 percent) gives to a Christian parachurch ministry—and roughly one-third of them never donate to a church. That reflects nearly 5 million households exclusively supporting parachurch ministries—and more than 9 out of 10 of those donors are believers.

The ministries that attracted the highest proportion of donors in 1996 were missionaries or missions groups that work overseas (61 percent of those who give to religious nonchurch ministries donated to such mission work) and youth ministries (45 percent). Two out of five supported social welfare ministries, while one out of every three donors gave to Christian parachurch agencies involved in discipleship, to Christian schools, colleges or other educational ministries, to Christian-based child sponsorship and to evangelistic organizations. Smaller percentages of donors to Christian organizations gave to media ministries and ministries focused on public policy or legal matters.[3]

These choices offer a significant revelation. The distribution of funds among these kinds of ministries often indicates the areas of ministry these donors believe are inadequately addressed by their church. Many of these parachurch donors would give their money to their church if they believed their church was doing a good job in a similar ministry. In many situations, we discovered that these gifts to parachurch groups reflected the difference in ministry priorities held by donors and church leaders. Do you know what kinds of parachurch ministries your people support, and why they support those specific organizations? Knowing the answer to these questions could provide valuable insight into how to fine-tune your ministry to gain greater involvement and greater funding.

Establishing Ministry Ownership

Have you ever noticed that in most successful small businesses the person who works the longest hours, takes on the greatest responsibility and exhibits the deepest passion for doing a job right is usually the owner? His commitment to doing whatever is necessary to ensure smooth and profitable operations is a testimony to the power of ownership.

PEOPLE WHO OWN THE MINISTRY FUND THE MINISTRY.

Enabling people in a church to believe they own the ministry is a crucial step in promoting the responsibility for ministry to be spread among the people. Ownership also upgrades people's financial commitment to their church. As owners, those in the pews shed their standing as spectators at a pleasant weekly event, or nominal members of a positive-values country club. Ownership transforms them into the ministers on whose shoulders the church lives or dies.

Perhaps facilitating congregational ownership of the ministry does not sound like a core fund-raising principle. It is, though. <u>Until the people of the church feel that they *are* the church, as opposed to feeling that they attend the church, their giving will be anemic</u>. Christians who are not wholeheartedly committed to the particular ministry may have great intentions in the realm of stewardship, but they are likely to lack the passion that stimulates extraordinary support of a cause, institution or individual.

Ownership usually evolves in an orderly fashion. I believe people move along a continuum, imperfectly and at different rates of growth, which leads them to eventually feel ownership of a church. Often the first step is for a person to attend the church's worship services. Once comfortable and satisfied with that experience, the person might then like the ministry well enough to call it his church "home." This entry-level commitment may pave the way to intellectually and emotionally accepting the church's mission, vision and values.

Having bought into the significance of the ministry, the next step usually is either volunteering around the church or beginning to give money regularly (although not tithing). At this stage, the person will then grow in terms of the time and energy committed to personal and corporate faith practices (e.g., Bible study groups, Bible reading, prayer, attending Christian education classes). When—and if—their faith becomes the central factor in their lives, they are likely to make the church the core of their personal spiritual journey. A few of these people may decide that part of their maturation as believers requires the privilege of tithing. Other forms of heightened commitment might follow (e.g., full-time ministry commitment) among those who are most fervent about their faith.

> **UNTIL THE PEOPLE OF THE CHURCH FEEL THAT THEY _ARE_ THE CHURCH, AS OPPOSED TO FEELING THAT THEY _ATTEND_ THE CHURCH, THEIR GIVING WILL BE ANEMIC.**

This progression suggests that for a church to raise up a battalion of tithers it must guide people into an ever-deepening relationship with Jesus, with other believers and with the church. Until potential donors truly own the church and its ministry, the chances of them tithing are limited. Ownership occurs when they have been exposed to and have had positive experiences with multiple dimensions of the ministry. Ownership is a virtual prerequisite to making a serious financial commitment to a church.

Proper Positioning

Positioning is the art of communicating targeted information about a product or concept to stake out a strategic place on the mental map of a person. Properly executed, positioning constitutes a blend of image and reality, style and substance. It represents the way in which you want someone to think of your product, service or idea.

Although positioning is second nature to seasoned marketers, it is foreign territory to most pastors and church staff. Consequently, most churches do not intentionally position their fund-raising and stewardship activities for their congregants. Instead, the congregants determine, by default, how the relationships between faith, money, lifestyle and church are positioned in their minds and hearts. Among churches that attempt to position these matters, the most common approach is to portray financial support and resource management as a response to the needs of the church. Yet this course of action almost always undermines the church because it focuses on the needs of the church rather than on the motivations of the donor.

> **REFER TO YOUR FUND-RAISING EFFORTS AS STEWARDSHIP; POSITION STEWARDSHIP AS THE MEANS OF FULFILLING A DONOR'S NEED TO PURPOSEFULLY CONTRIBUTE FUNDS.**

Thousands of churches are losing ground because they have failed to purposefully and strategically position their financial development efforts. A more pragmatic and effective way to approach fund-raising is to marry the biblical imperative (i.e., God commands us to behave responsibly with our resources, which includes returning a portion to Him for His purposes) and the individual felt need (i.e., to receive the joy of giving through the satisfaction of one's motivations). Ideally, this marriage is performed under the banner of stewardship (or a more user-friendly term that retains the meaning of biblically based resource management).

Because part of the church's mission is to transform believers into authentic, devoted disciples of Christ, equipping believers to understand their giving as one more step in the Christian maturation process is not only feasible, but also desirable. Fostering personal growth through giving, however, means that the emphasis must be on more than just percentages of income, frequency of giving and funding as a means to an operational end. The highly effective fund-raising churches go to great lengths to position all budgeting, fund-raising and related financial endeavors as a challenge to a person's lifestyle, theology and perspective.

If the congregation perceives the church's fund-raising efforts to be merely a game of reaching dollar goals or making the balance sheet zero out at the end of the fiscal year, then the church has failed. You can be confident that in God's eyes what is important is not how much money the church can raise or how many congregants get involved in the fund-raising effort, but the attitude of those to whom God has entrusted His earthly goods.

Appropriate positioning elements, then, might include the following:

- *Description of the activity:* "stewardship," meaning the strategic management of God's resources that have been entrusted to us.
- *Motivation for the activity:* obedience to God, love of God, ability to influence lives, the joy of doing what is right in God's eyes, participation in a win-win behavior.
- *Significance:* one of the most tangible signs of a transformed life, one of the biblical responsibilities assigned to believers.

Churches that are able to position their financial campaigns in this manner help people grow and experience less resistance to expanding financial needs within the ministry.

Providing Financial Data

Igniting and maintaining people's excitement and enthusiasm is no simple task in even the best of conditions. To do so in relation to giving, one of the secrets to success is to consistently communicate important information to people. A well-informed congregation leads to a well-endowed ministry.

> **AN UNINFORMED DONOR IS AN UNMOTIVATED DONOR.**

Your donors need more than an upbeat, perfunctory update about church finances. They must receive uplifting but realistic reports about the progress made during a stewardship campaign and throughout the fiscal year. Such reports should both encourage and challenge your people. Remember: people cannot own a ministry they do not understand, and people cannot understand it if they are not kept up to date about its status.

An examination of the communications within the most effective fund-raising churches found the following elements in common:

- *The messages are concise.* Church people are busy people. They do not have time for meandering, long-winded missives. It is hard enough to capture their attention. The best way to maximize it is to get to the point. Direct communications also increase the possibility of capturing the donor's attention in the future: People remember who respects their time and they respond accordingly.

- *The messages stress benefits delivered.* Donors want to know what value has been produced through their generosity. Communiqués that describe how people have been helped, nurtured or activated for ministry underscore the positive effect of donations made to the church. Reinforce donors' decisions to support the church by allowing them to hear some of the stories of life change that resulted from the ministry the donor has funded.

- *The messages describe progress made to achieve specific financial goals.* To encourage continued support, donors need to receive regular reports about how well the church is advancing toward its goal. Although most people do not set goals in their own lives, they do have some resonance with goals set by the groups to which they feel they belong (i.e., ownership). An active donor must be an informed donor.

- *The messages are honest and open.* Integrity is a necessity in all fund-raising efforts. If people sense they are not receiving the real story (i.e., they get only the positive information, they get only part of the story, there are hidden problems), then their commitment to giving will dissipate. Questions must be answered directly and honestly. Information about the current status and financial standing of the church must be simple and credible. Losing people's trust through deception is a failing from which the church may not recover for years and years.

- *Frequent communications.* If donors are to be partners, they must feel like insiders. The messages are more effective when they are frequent and brief than when they are infrequent and long-winded.

- *The church relies upon a mixture of communication vehicles.* If the communication process gets stuck in a rut, it loses its effect. The effective churches tend to convey important information through a wealth of channels: sermons, newsletters, the worship program, special congregational meetings, letters to donor households, planned personal encounters, a Web site on the Internet, the annual report, special inserts and platform announcements. Although it is useful to develop some standardization and predictability in the communication process, it is also imperative to avoid anesthetizing people with too much predictability or an abundance of routine. Keep them on their toes.

- *The messages are personalized.* As much as possible, the messages are customized to the needs and expectations of the people who are participating in the stewardship activities of the church. This personalization includes an allowance for—no, an expectation of—feedback and reaction from the audience. Our study found that although most messages are delivered in a mass medium format and to a large audience, there are occasional forays into interactive communication regarding stewardship, and regular, if infrequent, attempts at personalizing the information for the receiver.

Financial Information Provided

Beyond providing narrative descriptions of the church's financial status and progress, 9 out of every 10 Protestant churches also make available financial data in the form of balance sheets, budgets, salaries and contribution receipts. This is true regardless of the size of the church. The main difference among churches is the aggressiveness with which they get this information into the hands and minds of their donors.

A few churches have the information available upon request. A larger number make the information available for the taking, making it accessible, but not intentionally distributing it to congregants. The remaining churches mass distribute such documentation, seeking to give the information to each congregant. It appears that the preferred method of dissemination depends at least partially upon the church's style of government (e.g., presbyterian, congregational, episcopal).

A majority of churches that have budgets of $100,000 a year or more also print the previous week's giving totals in the Sunday bulletin. (Just less than half of the smallest churches—44 percent—follow this practice.)

Balancing Large and Small Gifts

The conventional wisdom in fund-raising is that 80 percent of the money comes from 20 percent of the donors. As we studied the workings of such churches, however, we found this to be an unhealthy condition. A church is better off if its funding base is spread much more democratically across the congregation.

Churches that operate in the 80-20 scenario often find that they become economic hostages to the whims and motives of the major donors. The sad truth is that people sometimes exchange their money—even if it is provided as a "gift"—for influence or power. Major donors who become the financial refuge of a church often expect something special in return for their disproportionate support: access to the pastor, decision-making influence or special treatment. The best way to avoid becoming captive to the dictates of a handful of "spiritual sugar daddies" is to be sure the church is not dependent upon one or just a handful of big givers.

> **CHURCHES THAT HEAVILY RELY UPON MAJOR DONORS ARE ECONOMIC HOSTAGES TO THOSE "SPIRITUAL SUGAR DADDIES."**

Nothing is wrong with strategically seeking large gifts or special designated donations. However, a majority of the pastors we interviewed who intentionally tap major donors recognize that it is dangerous to rely upon big gifts alone—or even primarily—to pull the church through tough times or special projects. Trade-offs are inherent in every relationship; the trade-offs may be most unhealthy when the exchange is based on large sums of money changing hands.

Thus, though it is reasonable to pursue major donors and seek large gifts from those people, the most important strategic element of a successful stewardship campaign is to raise money from a broad base of people. Small gifts may not be as exciting, but cumulatively they represent the fuel that energizes the ministry. A key to avoiding the necessity of unusually large donations is to set goals and develop ministries without the assumption of such gifts.

Expressing Appreciation

Most churches are not good at thanking their supporters. In dissecting the stewardship practices and procedures of churches, it seems that the main reasons for failing to show appreciation are the following:

- *Pastors expect people to give.* When people fulfill this expectation, signs of appreciation are often overlooked because giving is taken for granted.
- *Overt appreciation cheapens the gift.* Because our giving is supposed to reflect a heart filled with gratitude toward God for all He does for us, thanking people for their expression of love is sometimes thought of as trivializing the spiritual meaning of the gift.
- *Those who could express thanks do not know who gives.* In many churches, the only people who know the identity of donors are the staff or volunteers who send out end-of-year giving state-

ments, or who prepare the church's bank deposits. Consequently, the people who have the platform to offer thanks do not have the information to provide meaningful thanks. This reflects one of the great tensions involved in fund-raising: recognizing the graciousness of the donor versus maintaining confidentiality regarding generosity.

- *People should not need to be thanked.* The attitude behind this perspective is: "If people need to be thanked for giving, their motives are wrong and their donations are not gifts but bribes." Leaders who possess this attitude believe that giving is the people's duty, spending is the church's duty and thanking is God's responsibility. They contend that God thanks His people His way—by supernaturally instilling within donors peace and joy resulting from their selfless act.

CONSISTENT AND SINCERE EXPRESSIONS OF GRATITUDE MAY BE YOUR MOST EFFECTIVE REQUEST FOR FURTHER FUNDING.

These (and most other) excuses are weak, at best. Providing a heartfelt and appropriate show of appreciation to those who give to the church reinforces people's decisions to give, models Christian graciousness, enhances donors' sense of ownership of the ministry and builds loyalty to the community within the church. The failure to express appreciation undermines the values on which biblical stewardship is based and misses an opportunity to deepen people's commitment to stewardship.

Notes
1. Jerold Panas, *Born to Raise* (Chicago: Pluribus Press, 1988), p. 3.
2. Understanding and communicating God's vision for the ministry of your church is one of the most important factors in effective ministry. There is no viable substitute for God's vision; it operates as the cornerstone of ministry, and a catalyst to people's understanding and ownership of the ministry. For a more detailed discussion about what vision is, how it differs from mission and how to discern vision, refer to *The Power of Vision* by George Barna (Ventura, Calif.: Regal Books, 1992). To gain insight into how to convert the vision into practical and powerful ministry, see *Turning Vision into Action* by George Barna (Ventura, Calif.: Regal Books, 1996).
3. These figures are based on data from OmniPoll 1-96, January 1996, N=1004, conducted by the Barna Research Group, Ltd.

8

Segmenting the Donor Base

"THE DILEMMA FOR MANY PEOPLE IS THAT THEY GIVE THE WIDOW'S MITE BUT NOT WITH THE WIDOW'S SPIRIT."

ANONYMOUS

Often churches set their financial goals on the basis of what they have raised in the past. This creates a major difficulty. Budgets dictated by past fund-raising performance can only grow incrementally, if at all. The assumption is that people are giving what they think they can, and at best the church can only push them a little bit more.

Successful churches refuse to be limited by the past; they take another tack. They analyze the ability of the church to give and then set their sights accordingly. This is a much more daring approach because it heightens the possibility of failing to meet goals. However, it also raises the performance bar higher because the goals are tied to capacity rather than history, assumptions and fear. Given the biblical standards for giving many churches promote, this strategy is more in line with a faith-based process for fund-raising.

Setting goals according to capacity also differentiates between people's *desire* to give, their *ability* to give and their actual *giving*. In essence, evaluating according to these three delineators facilitates developing a financial capacity study, similar to those a lending institution might develop before approving a loan to an organization or individual. Armed with such data, a church can then set its sights on what the congregation is able to give (allowing for the need for personal growth) and plan its campaign accordingly.

A Segmentation Plan

Effective fund-raising churches refuse to treat all people as equals—and people truly are not when it comes to giving. Potential donors may be distinguished in various ways: the will to give, the ability to give, past giving performance, loyalty to the ministry and commitment to biblical stewardship principles. Most of these churches develop some kind of segmentation strategy in which they categorize the congregation into types of donors.

> **IT IS FRUITFUL TO DIFFERENTIATE BETWEEN PEOPLE'S *DESIRE* TO GIVE, THEIR *ABILITY* TO GIVE AND THEIR ACTUAL *GIVING*.**

The segmentation concept is an old one. Some professional fund-raisers refer to Benjamin Franklin as the oldest proponent of such a strategy. Franklin was an advocate of Pennsylvania Hospital, one of the few medical care providers in the Philadelphia area during the late 1700s. Franklin used to spend many hours seeking to raise money from leading citizens to maintain and develop the hospital. He is the first person we can identify who solicited funds for nonchurch institutions from individuals, rather than relying upon the government to fund a public-interest entity. Franklin wrote about his formula for raising money.

> My practice is to go first to those who may be counted upon to be favorable, who know the cause and believe in it, and ask them to give as generously as possible. When I have done so I go next to those who may be presumed to have a favorable opinion and to be disposed to listening, and I secure their adherence. Lastly, I go to those who know little of the matter or have no known predilection for it and influence them by the presentation of the names of those who have already given.[1]

> **SEGMENTATION ESTABLISHES PRIORITIES THAT ENABLE YOU TO USE YOUR FUND-RAISING RESOURCES MORE EFFICIENTLY.**

Franklin also wrote about the different strategies he used with the people from these groups, tailoring his pitch to the needs or interests the prospective donor might have in supporting the hospital.

Creating a Church Segmentation Strategy

Based on our research, we have discovered several kinds of donors to churches. It is possible to develop a segmentation strategy unique to a given church because the congregations of churches vary. Our experience has shown, however, that if the proper variables related to attitudes, giving ability and past giving history are examined, most church people fall into one of five categories. Several churches have adopted these categories to develop more targeted fund-raising efforts. The following is a brief description of the categories we have found.

• *Misers.* See Ebenezer Scrooge (before his conversion). These people rarely give away money. When they do, it is a difficult moment for them. Their gifts are usually less than two dollars. On those rare occasions when they give, they do so grudgingly. The notion of stewardship as a matter of spiritual obedience is a foreign concept to Misers. The idea of being a cheerful giver seems ridiculous to them.

MISERS ARE OBLIVIOUS TO THE CONCEPT OF BIBLICAL STEWARDSHIP.

Misers do not view donating as an investment, nor do they have a high appreciation for the work of nonprofit organizations or churches. They tend to think they earned their money and if others want it, they should earn it. Discussions about money are difficult for them; finances are a private matter in their view. They marvel at the generosity of philanthropists—not because they are impressed with their compassion, but dumbfounded by the stupidity of people giving away their cash.

How do you recognize a Miser? Can you think of a few people in your congregation who give a quarter or dollar every Christmas or Easter, without fail, and never let you forget that they are consistent supporters of the church? Do you have a cadre of people who wince and grimace every time the offering plate comes around, or who complain that the church talks and focuses too much on money? Chances are, those are your Misers.

Misers can become more consistent and more generous church donors, but it takes a long-term, relational strategy. It requires tremendous diligence and generally does not benefit from repeated Scripture references. These folks need to be softened all around; the issues they are battling go deeper than that of hoarding their money. That behavior tends to be a symptom of a deeper struggle.

• *Penny Pinchers.* These people acknowledge that giving is a good thing to do, but they remain oblivious to the notion that the amount they contribute makes a difference in the breadth and depth of influence achieved by their support. In their minds they are virtuous because they give regularly. Penny Pinchers typically donate a few dollars each week to their church, and they may even throw a few coins into the Salvation Army bucket at Christmas. It is unusual for them to write a check of any size for any other kind of organization or individual need. The data suggest that Catholics are most commonly in this category.

PENNY PINCHERS BELIEVE THEY ARE VIRTUOUS PEOPLE BECAUSE THEY GIVE REGULARLY TO A CHURCH.

Realize that in spite of the pejorative label associated with people in this segment, these are not necessarily greedy people. For instance, single-parent mothers often fall into this category. Most of these women have fallen on hard times subsequent to a divorce and are on the edge financially. They are willing to donate to the church, but are not likely to be receptive to appeals to increase their level of commitment. Many of these women are in a survival mode economically. Widows are often in this segment.

Penny Pinchers who are not in a survival mode economically can be converted into better donors if they comprehend the significance of the spirit of giving. These folks are often legalistic in nature and interpret Scriptures related to stewardship as focusing upon regularity rather than generosity. Helping them realize that God is interested in the heart behind the gift often unleashes the purse strings. Helping them view their giving as an investment is another useful and appropriate strategy with many of these people. They have been giving from a sense of duty or obligation, rather than from a sense of influence or joy. They typically need a theological corrective.

ALTRUISTS DO NOT BELIEVE THAT GIVING TO CHURCHES IS GOOD STEWARDSHIP; THEY DO NOT SEE A COMPELLING OUTCOME.

• *Altruists.* These folks believe in doing what they can to improve the quality of life and the condition of society. They give significant amounts of money to nonprofit organizations that champion causes in which they believe. However, Altruists do not give money to churches. They believe that churches do spiritual work; charitable organizations and other nonprofits do the kind of global enhancement activity that requires private support. Many Altruists attend churches; they simply choose to channel their funds through other networks of influence.

Altruists are sometimes the most vocal and tireless social activists. One reason they may eschew giving to a church is that many churches—including theirs—have an anemic community outreach ministry.

Although they possess a willingness and an ability to give consistently and generously, they are often difficult to convert into church donors. In their minds, they have already found the causes that are meaningful and transformational. They generally do not perceive theological change (e.g., conversion, worldview shifts) as the kind of practical transformation that justifies their money. Moving these folks from the Altruist category to a more valued category often requires a change in the church's ministry: enhancing the social outreach programs, involving the Altruist in those programs or convincingly demonstrating life change resulting from the church's ministry. It also requires a new understanding of biblical stewardship as including the work of the church.

• *Zealots.* These givers believe that if they are to donate funds, it should be to a church that will do good works in the name of God. They appreciate the work of parachurch groups and other nonprofit charities, but they funnel their contributions through their church, alone. They are usually relatively steady and prolific givers—people who may not tithe (although many do), but who make a serious annual commitment to support the efforts of their church. Zealots give through their church because they have confidence in its integrity; they believe they remain close to their investment; and they tend to embrace the biblical admonition to give to their church.

**ZEALOTS ARE STEADY, CONSISTENT GIVERS—
BUT NOT TITHERS.**

This segment is sensitive about appeals to upgrade their giving. They perceive themselves to be doing more than others in the church are doing and thus feel they should be applauded, not "upsold." A successful upgrade process often includes an emphasis on the significance of the cause represented by the church, and an understanding of urgent needs that must be met in the lives of people groups that are important to Zealots.

• *Investors.* Many donors believe in the work of the church, but want to broaden their influence to touch on aspects of need their church does not address. Thus, these people also donate to nonprofits other than their church. They tend to be more generous than the average person, often giving away 10 percent or more of their income, but not exclusively to a church. Usually a tiny segment of church-only tithers is part of a typical congregation. Increasingly, though, we are discovering a growing number of tithers within churches who wish to reduce their "risk" by investing in a variety of worthy organizations.

> **INVESTORS: THESE FOLKS TITHE, BUT THEIR ENTIRE 10 PERCENT MAY NOT GO TO THE CHURCH.**

In my travels, I have found that churches sometimes develop their own segmentation categories based on a strategy they have conceived for raising ministry funds. The important factor is not which segmentation strategy you use, but whether or not the one you use works within the context of your stewardship endeavors. Because segmentation must be used deftly (i.e., you do not want people to feel as if they have been slighted or demeaned on the basis of the segment in which they have been placed), it is crucial that you have a holistic approach to stewardship in which segmentation plays a significant role. Segmentation for its own sake, or for the sake of sophistication, is bad stewardship.

The Goals of Segmentation

Based on the segments described, our research has demonstrated that these categories are usually exhaustive and inclusive. One of the tasks of the fund-raising team is to determine what kinds of donors are present within the church and how to motivate them appropriately to donate to the church. Some people seem impervious to upgrading, so accurately identifying which category a potential donor fits within may help you avoid wasting resources on seeking to upgrade people's commitment. Those people may not be at a life stage, spiritual state or economic condition to give significantly to their church.

> **EFFECTIVE SEGMENTATION MOVES A PERSON FROM ONE CATEGORY TO ANOTHER, RAISING THE LEVEL OF COMMITMENT IN GIVING.**

Segmentation underscores stewardship as a process. It recognizes people for where they are and dares to challenge people to a higher—and hopefully biblical—standard of generosity. Adults typically move from one step on the continuum to the next; they do not usually jump from being a Miser to being an Investor in one season. Sometimes that occurs, but more often the person needs to test the waters and climb the ladder: Miser to Penny Pincher to Zealot to Investor. (Naturally, you try to avoid getting people into the Altruist category.)

I encountered a few churches who segmented their segments. For instance, they might divide a segment such as the Penny Pinchers into those who are economically incapable of giving more and those who are emotionally or psychologically resistant despite having the economic means. This finer delineation within segments can further fine-tune the fund-raising efforts.

We also know from the research that although we might like to think of tithing as an immediate addendum to a person's spiritual commitment to Christ, the reality is that tithing is more often an outgrowth of a developmental process. Thus, a person who has accepted Jesus Christ as his or her Savior and regularly attends church may not tithe or give generously to the work of the church at this moment.

> ### THE BEST DONORS ARE USUALLY THE VOLUNTEERS.

That person, however, may consistently but sensitively be challenged to consider biblical principles regarding stewardship, and witness friends and other respected people within the church give generously. This may help to eventually reach the point at which the person will give in a significant way. Patience and prayer are the order of the day for this kind of person because tithing or major giving does not automatically accompany the acceptance of salvation by grace.

Volunteers As Donors

We know, too, that the people who are involved in ministry activities almost always donate to their church. Recruiting people to become active ministry participants is a positive strategy for encouraging people to donate to the church. Serving the ministry in a volunteer capacity not only enables them to experience the privilege and fulfillment of personal ministry, but also constitutes a soft way of leading them to donate funds to the ministry. Those who support the church through their volunteer efforts generally develop a greater degree of ownership of the ministry than do people who simply attend and take advantage of what the church has to offer.

Volunteers typically have a greater awareness of the needs the church is addressing and of the ministry's influence within the congregation and the community. Many volunteers graduate from the ranks of the minor donors to the level of significant contributor, a shift attributable to their newfound understanding of the immensity of the needs and the positive prospects for influence through the work of the church.

Treating Unequal Donors Unequally

One of the controversial philosophies in raising money for churches is that of recognizing that all donors do not possess equal financial value to the church. Although it is undeniable that in Christ we are all equal "for you are all one in Christ Jesus" (Gal. 3:28), when it comes to raising money we cannot maximize our potential by expecting equal gifts from everyone.

People who earn relatively large sums of money or who have more disposable wealth have generally reached that place in life because of their unique understanding and perspectives related to money and wealth. Communicating effectively with them often requires that they be approached differently and handled differently. They typically respond to different kinds of appeals and opportunities than do people of lesser means. The approach to them should be handled intelligently, sensitively and fully cognizant of the spiritual parameters within which we must work when we raise money for ministry.

Realize that we are not to esteem wealthy or major donors any more highly than those people who give smaller donations that are no less significant a sacrifice, given their personal abilities. The parable of the widow's mite is an effective lesson about Jesus' perspective on levels of giving. The money donated by the affluent, no matter how large in sum, is not more precious or significant than the $5 a week donated by the widow who ekes out a modest living on her social security check. By virtue of how God has blessed each of them financially, and the knowledge they possess of the workings of wealth, it is reasonable to communicate with potential major donors in a different way to enable them to give as they are called to give.

The Disclaimer

A relatively recent phenomenon has been the practice of churches telling visitors they need not feel an obligation to contribute to the offering because they are the guests of the church.[2] One-quarter of all churches communicate such a disclaimer during their services. This group includes many churches that neither have a "seeker service" nor are striving to be "seeker driven" ministries. These disclaimers are wise positioning, though.

The purpose of the disclaimer statement is to defuse people's skepticism or fear regarding churches' emphasis upon money, or to diminish their perception that the church is more interested in people's giving than in the people who are giving. From a positioning standpoint this practice is brilliant; it redirects people's attention from peripheral issues to core considerations regarding monetary matters. My informal conversations with many pastors indicate that few who use the disclaimer have a reliable means of determining the effect of this tactic. Intuitively, however, you can imagine the qualitative edge gained by such a positioning tactic.

A discussion of disclaimers, though, must be balanced by a discussion of how to educate visitors to recognize when they are no longer "off the hook." Most churches include a discussion of stewardship and giving in the introductory classes or meetings attended by visitors who want to join the church or learn more about how the church operates and whether or not the church might be right for them. It is imperative to provide a clear presentation at that time to alert potential congregants to the realities of stewardship. The sooner their education in this regard takes place, the better; waiting too long may give people the impression that they were victims of a "bait and switch" operation in which the economic realities of the relationship were unfairly withheld.

Notes

1. Jerold Panas, *The Official Fund Raising Almanac* (Chicago: Pluribus Press, 1989), p. 61.
2. The typical disclaimer goes something like this: "Now we come to that time in our service when we take an offering. If you are visiting with us today, please feel no obligation or pressure to participate in this part of the service. You are our guest and we are pleased that you are with us today. Sit back, relax and enjoy your experience here. This portion of our service is when those of us who call this church our spiritual home get to worship God by returning to Him some of what He has blessed us with, to support this ministry."

9

Marketing Church Stewardship

"PEOPLE GIVE TO A WINNING CAUSE,

NOT TO A SINKING SHIP."

KENNON CALLAHAN

A decade ago I wrote a book about ministry, which was innocently—or, more accurately, naively—titled *Marketing the Church*. Apparently nobody had previously been bold enough to suggest that the church gets marketed. Amid the hailstorm of criticism that followed the release and promotion of the book, I found out why I was "credited" with blazing the church marketing trail: My predecessors had been too smart to call church marketing by that term. As I soon realized, the giants of church marketing on whose shoulders I thought I was standing had referred to "church marketing" by using code names such as "ministry development," "church growth," "community relations," "marketplace outreach" and, for the truly courageous, "church promotion."

Upon interacting with some of my rational critics—and more than a few whose outrage at the mere suggestion that churches or any ministry activity are marketed were disqualified from this group—I discovered that the discomfort generated by the title of my book was based on a basic misunderstanding of what marketing is all about and what it entails. After a calm and logical discussion, I found that most of my critics were still uncomfortable admitting they are marketing the church, but acknowledged they do engage in acts of marketing.

"Marketing," in some circles, has a bad name. It implies manipulation, deception and excessive control. In reality, marketing is not a bad thing at all; it has no ethical content other than that which that marketer brings. Marketing simply refers to all the activities designed to result in a transaction in which commodities of equal value are exchanged. It entails a variety of common and ethically appropriate activities such as advertising, promotions, sales, database management, product development, distribution, audience research and so forth.

When marketing is characterized by some of the excesses mentioned, that is an abuse of an honorable activity, just as we can have abusive leadership or inefficient management. Bad practice does not negate the utility and value of a discipline. In its true form, marketing provides a benefit to both parties involved in the transaction.

> **THE REAL QUESTION IS NOT WHETHER OR NOT A CHURCH MARKETS THE ELEMENTS OF ITS MINISTRY, BUT HOW WELL DOES IT MARKET THOSE ELEMENTS?**

Churches constantly engage in marketing through activities as simple as placing an ad in the Yellow Pages or as complex as communicating a special event targeted to teenagers through the Internet. The typical church markets virtually every aspect of its ministry, from the children's Sunday School classes to the women's prayer circle, from the community outreach event to the Sunday morning worship service. The real question is not whether or not a church markets the elements of its ministry, but how well does it market those elements? As in everything else we do in the name of ministry, and for the purposes of Christ, we must do those things with excellence because ultimately we are serving God through those actions (see Col. 3:23). He deserves nothing less than our best.

In our complex and diverse marketplace, the competition for people's attention and resources is not other churches. Few people ponder how to divide their time and energy among a set of worthy church alternatives. More often, people compare the pros and cons of church involvement with the advantages and disadvantages accrued from engaging in other activities, causes, organizations and opportunities resident within the marketplace. Consequently, the quality of a church's marketing may make or break its ministry.[1]

Effective fund-raising churches include their stewardship campaigns among the ever-growing list of ministry ventures that must be well marketed if they are to succeed. How do those churches market stewardship?

Creating an Attractive Image

People donate to winners. As they evaluate the many options to which they could provide financial support, donors are searching for evidence of an organization's victories or its undeniable potential to become a winner. Donors need to see a track record, especially if they are seeking to be good stewards (i.e., they must invest God's money wisely, which is often translated to mean they must find and support ministries that have made a difference, or are likely to).

> **"THE CAUSE MUST CATCH THE EYE, WARM THE HEART AND STIR THE MIND." HAROLD SEYMOUR**

Jesus once instructed a crowd of followers that it is not appropriate to light a lamp and then place that lamp under a bowl (see Matt. 5:14-16). He appears to be speaking about living a righteous life. He specifically suggests that if we have followed His teachings and have lived a righteous life, and have done so for God's glory, we should let others know of this commitment and countercultural behavior so that they may realize how God is at work within us and, as a result, give praise to God.

The same principle can be applied to how a church informs its people of the praiseworthy things that have happened in the lives of the people to whom the church has ministered. How can God be honored and glorified if we are bashful about describing how He has ministered through us and thereby transformed people's lives? Is conveying such information bragging? It could be, of course, if we take the credit for the good works or if we exaggerate their influence. If we are merely reciting the marvelous ways in which He has chosen to use us, as His hands and feet in the world, and if we tell the story with all due respect and humility, then proclaiming His good works is anything but conceit!

> **IF WE ARE MERELY RECITING THE MARVELOUS WAYS IN WHICH HE HAS CHOSEN TO USE US, AS HIS HANDS AND FEET IN THE WORLD, AND IF WE TELL THE STORY WITH ALL DUE RESPECT AND HUMILITY, THEN PROCLAIMING HIS GOOD WORKS IS ANYTHING BUT CONCEIT!**

This means that your church must decide how to maintain an acceptable level of modesty while concurrently "tooting its own horn" regarding its ministry influence. Reporting your "victories" is not a brazen act of self-promotion, but merely an exercise in honest communication. You need not amplify your track record to the point of distortion; you must simply make that record accessible to the people who need and want to know about it.

Reminding the congregation of the ways the church has been used by God as an instrument of blessing to other people is a difficult practice for some church leaders to accept. Their assumption is that if you simply tell the Body about the *needs* of the church, their tender hearts and spiritual discernment will result in an outpouring of donations. This thinking is emotionally seductive; we would like to think the best of our people, and assume that we need not engage in strategic actions that will motivate them. After all, that is God's job, isn't it?

As alluring as this thinking might be, it is wrong. The apostle Paul consistently demonstrated the need to keep God's people informed by writing letters to his churches, updating them on new outcomes, instructing them about misunderstood principles and challenging them to change errant behaviors and interpretations of Scripture. Paul wrote, "I do not want you to be misinformed" (see 1 Cor. 10:1; 12:1; 2 Cor. 1:8; 1 Thess. 4:13). He recognized the importance of a proper perspective on what God has done and continues to do through us.

Further, the practical side of stewardship in modern society underscores the reality that people must be motivated to give away their money; it doesn't just happen. Nothing is inappropriate about providing congregants with compelling, accurate motivations for donating to the church. Theologically, expecting God's people to give without providing the facts for them is to ask them to reject biblical stewardship in favor of empty emotionalism.

Part of our teaching about stewardship is to accept our biblical responsibilities in conjunction with an honest assessment of the opportunities available to us. We cannot reasonably ask congregants to ignore the principles they have been taught simply because we do not want the church to have to live up to its end of the stewardship equation.

People are generous, but they are also surprisingly cautious about how they give away their money. The typical American loses no sleep over wasting cash on frivolous activities that bring fleeting, momentary joy, but has a natural resistance to indiscriminately giving money to nonprofit organizations—including to those whose work might result in a positive social influence or reap spiritual dividends for God's kingdom. Literally millions of church people will never give their church anything more than pocket change unless they become convinced that the church has the potential to make a difference and that it will minister at a high level of quality.

Thus, to most effectively raise the money you need, you must appropriately publicize the record of ministry accomplishments attributable to the church. Potential donors are likely to respond favorably to a compelling vision of the future, but unless the individual or organization promoting that vision has a viable track record to back up the vision, it sounds like pious dreams and fantasies.

In an age when only 7 percent of all donors say they have a lot of confidence in the integrity and competence of the leaders of nonprofit organizations, you have to purposefully build their confidence that their investment in the church will pay off handsomely. You may achieve that goal by showing that past investments have been wisely utilized and have borne impressive fruit.

Motivate by Describing Benefits

The American culture trains people to perform a cost-benefit analysis regarding the options available to us. In those calculations, we seek to determine the relative benefits we will receive from each possible course of action. This is true in most people's stewardship decisions as well. Effective fund-raising churches market to people expecting the benefits to be received as one element of the communications package.

Naturally, the church must walk a fine line between promoting giving that is designed to "earn" personal blessings and promoting giving that is motivated by selflessness. We must not lead our people to think that by giving back to God what is already His we deserve and will automatically receive tangible rewards. On the other hand, if we seek to motivate people by appealing solely to their purity of heart, we will be addressing a limited audience.

Like Europeans and others from the developed nations of the world, Americans fear being "taken" by scams, inferior products and inequitable deals. They are skeptical of all who approach them with a good opportunity, whether it is a good opportunity to achieve a ministry outcome or a good opportunity to achieve a lifestyle outcome.

Undeniably, our giving is not meant for the purpose of extorting blessings from God. Yet Scripture also informs us that God blesses those who are faithful in their giving. Thus, if your congregants possess a good understanding of properly motivated generosity and God's benevolent response, you have done your people the grand service of translating stewardship to the realm of spiritual discipline and personal relevance. To strike that balance demands that you fully contextualize your financial requests without compromising the biblical principles on which your ministry is based. There is never, of course, a viable justification for redefining God's truths—including the ability to raise more money, even if that money results in more extensive and commendable forms of ministry.

Keep this in mind: Donors are consumers at heart. Like you, they live in a consumer-oriented society. To my great chagrin, 15 years of research experience has proven to me that the vast majority of Christians in America think and act like consumers first, Christians second. As church leaders, we do not have to like that reality, but we must recognize that it is the reality.

In practical terms, this means we must help donors see the church in its best light, and within a relevant context. What is that context? The typical donor likes to give to *growing* organizations. He prefers supporting entities that have high potential for positive *influence*. He is most likely to be drawn to outfits that do high *quality* work. The typical donor also seeks organizations that exude *credibility and integrity*.

Most churches are able to satisfy those criteria, yet many of those qualified churches do not stimulate the donor to give. Why not? Because the church has failed to intentionally, honestly and completely present its case to the donor. That is not the fault of the donor; it is the fault of those who are marketing the church's ministry to the donor.

When it comes time to raise funds for your ministry, do not be bashful. Be humble, to be sure, but straightforward about the tremendous outcomes the church has produced, through the enablement of the Holy Spirit, in the most recent funding cycle. Put your best foot forward.

If you have good reason to anticipate your church will grow numerically, do not ask people to give because the growth will require more staff, additional parking spaces, new books for children in Sunday School or increased money to print materials. Portray that growth in terms of the spiritual needs such growth will unleash and allow people to joyfully and expectantly invest in those potential benefits for the church.

If your church expects to significantly improve the quality of its ministry, provide a detailed accounting of what that will look like and how such enhancements will upgrade the aggregate ministry. Whatever your church expects to do bigger, better or more impressively than before, show people why their help is necessary to make that desirable growth possible. Convey the need for money in terms of ministry effect, not in relation to organizational development or structural expansion.

MANY QUALIFIED CHURCHES DO NOT STIMULATE THE DONOR TO GIVE, BECAUSE THE CHURCH HAS FAILED TO INTENTIONALLY, HONESTLY AND COMPLETELY PRESENT ITS CASE TO THE DONOR.

What if you are at a church that does not have an impressive record? What if it has been a church on the decline and your desire is to raise the necessary money to halt the collapse and begin a restructuring and rebuilding process? First, be sure the church is salvageable. Like everything else in life, a church has a life cycle and you may simply be looking at an entity whose useful life has expired. That is not bad. Recognizing this reality is one of the best things that can happen to the people of the church, as long as they are then integrated into other vibrant church homes so they can remain growing, serving Christians.

If, however, the conclusion is that God (as opposed to the pastor or people) undeniably means for the church to continue, then two primary steps are crucial.

Initially, cut back all unnecessary activities to the point that the church is simply doing those things it can do well and effectively. People are much more likely to give to a ministry that does a few things superbly than to a church that does many things inadequately.

Then, provide a detailed, long-term plan to the congregation for how the church will be able to grow in the years ahead. People do not mind taking one step back, temporarily, if you can show them that such a regrouping is a necessary precursor to running forward for years to come. Especially in a context of past failure or disappointment, the people need to believe that the future will be more than a repeat of a discouraging past; they need to see the potential and the likelihood for victory.[2]

High Profile, High Intensity

An effective stewardship effort requires a careful and strategic approach to maximize the congregation's buy-in of the ministry and its budgetary needs. Our research suggests that three elements must be in place.

First, the leader must actively campaign on a consistent basis for the funds. Many churches have a pastor or other leader who is embarrassed to ask for funds, or who makes the request and then recedes into the shadows, hoping that people will remember and respond with gusto. Effective church stewardship campaigns, however, are no different from effective political election campaigns. The leader must be in the forefront and incite people to act, give them due cause to respond as he or she desires, and provide for them a credible and compelling perspective of the need for and probable outcomes stemming from their responses. The effective stewardship directors maintain a high profile until the goals of the campaign are met.

Second, the person heading the campaign must use the power of personal touch to raise money. People give to people. The credibility of personal relationships, combined with the appeal of strong leadership, encourages people to part with their money. The leader of the church's fund-raising efforts must be in constant contact with people to encourage them to give. This does not mean the director of the stewardship effort must make all the personal contacts; most of those should be delegated to appropriate assistants. The director must, however, capitalize on the emotional bonds that exist within the congregation as well as take advantage of people's warm feelings about the good work being accomplished by God through the church.

Stewardship is not effective when it relies solely upon educating people about the church's balance sheet; that is an intellectual game that will hurt the church's ability to raise the money it needs. Effective fund-raising touches people's hearts as well as satisfies their minds.

PEOPLE GIVE TO PEOPLE. THERE IS NO SUBSTITUTE FOR THE PERSONAL TOUCH, AND FOR STORIES THAT RELATE THE HUMANITY OF OUR MINISTRY.

Third, the leader must maintain a high level of visibility during the stewardship period. Regularly seeing and hearing from the leader is a continual reminder that the church is striving to meet some serious financial goals, and that every person who is part of the church has an important (if unequal) role to play. This visibility is not designed to make people feel guilty, but to remind them of their responsibility as part of the church Body.

Familiarity Breeds Generosity

Sometimes it is counterproductive to be predictable. For instance, one pastor I know preached on the same basic theme every week for a year. His contention was that the people so badly needed to hear the message that he intended to preach it enough times so it would never escape their consciousness. The people had a different analysis of their condition. They agreed that they needed to hear the message—once, maybe even twice. After the fifth message on the same theme, when it became painfully clear that this pastor's needle was stuck in one groove, attendance started a slow but steady and discernible decline.

Undaunted, the pastor fearlessly plunged forward, asserting that their unwillingness to be exposed to the message was evidence he was getting through to them and they were now having to confront their guilt, weakness and fallibility. In reality, they were merely conveying to him that he was too predictable, which meant he was no longer providing sufficient respect and value to justify their commitment.

When it comes to initiating a stewardship campaign, though, familiarity fosters comfort more often than it breeds contempt. If the church integrates stewardship into the ministry mentality it proposes for congregational adoption, the campaign is a culmination of a year's worth of preparation rather than a dreaded obligation they must fulfill.

Laziness in fund-raising is common. Thousands of churches have marshaled their resources for a fund-raising effort one year, then tried to live off the resulting momentum for the next several years. They think about stewardship the same way Joan Rivers refers to housework. "I hate housework. You make the beds, you do the dishes—and then six months later you have to start all over again."

Unfortunately, donors do not behave in a manner that would allow such a reliance upon past activities. Donors need to be constantly reminded and motivated to take their financial duties to the church seriously. Even in churches in which stewardship is a mentality, rather than an annual campaign or event, such a harvesting vehicle is still required to bring closure to their discoveries, intentions and desired commitment. Given all we know about potential church donors, it is the foolish church leader who assumes that donors will enthusiastically maintain (or increase) their financial commitments to the church from year to year without a serious, concerted effort to justify generous giving.

A church that recognizes it will be conducting a new campaign each year will begin to conceptualize ways throughout the year in which sermons, programs, activities, events and other endeavors will subtly incorporate the need for people to generously underwrite the work of the church. Such a church will also be more likely to perceive stewardship efforts and accountability as a necessary component of the ongoing ministry, rather than to perceive it to be a special project removed from the essence of the church's ministry or from the heart of the personal spiritual development of people.

Ideally, people's giving will become more of a permanent desire than simply a knee-jerk response to a campaign. When people embrace a stewardship mentality, not just a stewardship reaction, one of the ministry benefits is that they have moved a step closer to understanding that ministry is not about techniques and duties, but about a heart devoted to serving God and fulfilling His calling for each of us.

Quantifying the Outcomes

Churches that have effectively marketed their stewardship needs typically incorporate yet another element: measurement. To convince people to give generously, an objective means must be in place to determine if their investment being requested is intended for plausible outcomes.

When you describe the ministry goals people's money will facilitate, be sure those goals are measurable. Describing desirable outcomes that are not objectively measurable inevitably comes back to haunt the church. Talking about "seeing people mature in their faith" or "having a positive influence on the community" are ambiguous, virtually meaningless statements. Reliance upon narrative evidence is also a tough sell: People cannot negate the fact that a life here or there has been touched, but the weight of such evidence is less than that of a more systematic measurement.

As you conceive the stewardship appeal, develop assessment criteria that can be easily implemented and provide credible information that can be used as standards for determining ministry value.

Notes

1. For a more extensive discussion of the definitions, theories and practical applications of marketing in a church context, you may wish to examine my updated text *A Step-by-Step Guide to Church Marketing* (Ventura, Calif.: Regal Books, 1992); or *Marketing for Congregations* by Norman Sawchuck, Phillip Kotler et. al. (Nashville: Abingdon Press, 1994).

2. In a prior research study among churches that had been strong, but experienced an extended period of serious decline, then made a comeback, I learned that pruning is a key to restoring health. A church that is spread too thinly across many ministries it is not equipped to handle is doing nobody a great service. The most effective growth strategy is to cut back on the unnecessary or unfruitful branches of ministry, regain strength, and then evaluate the need to reinvigorate some of those former ministry endeavors. For more insight of this strategy for renewal, you may wish to peruse my book recapping our research: *Turnaround Churches* (Ventura, Calif.: Regal Books, 1993).

10

Leadership in Stewardship

"NEVER MISTAKE MOTION FOR ACTION."

ERNEST HEMINGWAY

Garry Wills has defined leadership as the art of "mobilizing others toward a goal shared by the leader and followers." Our research has demonstrated that stewardship is critically affected by the quality of leadership exhibited in the church, overall, as well as in relation to the stewardship efforts of the church, specifically. Effective leadership is not merely a necessity to allow a church to make progress in ministry; it is also a necessary selling point for fund-raising in a church.

Leadership Donors Expect

Churches often teach or encourage their people to think of stewardship as the practice of intelligent investing, seeking to gain a reasonable return on their investment. To realize such a gain, the donor must evaluate the mission, the plans and the activities undertaken by the ministry. When a church gives evidence of having significant reasons for existence, and makes serious inroads into its plans, an investor may take greater comfort in the wisdom of investing in that ministry. These positive outcomes are attributable to effective leadership.

As people consider the fund worthiness of a church, the most overt factor people evaluate is the quality of church leadership. People's lives are regularly affected by the nature and quality of that leadership. When it comes to considering the prospect of giving to a church, we discovered that potential donors tend to search for evidence of seven key attributes as indicators of viability. The following is a brief description of those attributes.

Vision
Vision is providing people with a preferable and compelling portrait of the future to which they may then devote themselves. The vision must be promoted consistently and passionately by the primary leaders of the church, and should stand as the core perspective from which ministry decisions are made. Vision is the element that gives people hope for the future—even if the present condition is satisfying. To encourage people to give generously, the leaders of the congregation must provide the church with a detailed and realistic picture of a preferable future. This picture permits God's people to be agents of life transformation in ways that resonate with their gifts, desires, opportunities and abilities.

Integrity
Most of us have fallen prey to the persuasive power of deceptive salesmen or presenters. Americans have built a high level of resistance to the charms and spells of smooth, professional communicators. People are searching for signs of integrity in the leaders of our churches. Does the leader follow through on his stated intentions or promises? Does he exaggerate stories or statistics, or does he tell it the way it really is? Does he live consistently with the lessons he teaches? Congregants need visual and experiential assurance that the people overseeing the financial matters of the church are beyond reproach. When they sense purity and reliability in their leaders, and are comfortable with the apparent motives behind their actions, then they are open to investing in the work of those people.

Credibility
An investment requires an understanding of the enterprise being funded. Potential donors may be attracted to a leader on an emotional level, and may be willing to listen to the teaching and ideas pronounced by that person. Providing financial support, though, is another matter altogether. An effective leader must describe realistic ministry plans, offer plausible information and situational analyses, and come with a proven track record of promises and subsequent performance.

Competence
When evaluating the suitability of an investment, church donors examine how well the leadership has served the people through its decision making, through its planning, through the quality of its operational management and on the proficiency and quantity of communication with the congregation.

The leaders of the church will serve as the stewards for the stewards; therefore, the prospective donor typically strives to determine how competent the leaders of the church have been in fulfilling their past responsibilities.

Enthusiasm

If the leaders are simply going about business as usual, the potential supporter is not likely to be turned on by the ministry. Donors need to believe they are giving to something that is more significant than survival, more exciting than just a job, more influential than institutional religious practice. Church leaders who exude such a high level of belief in the ministry and enthusiasm about what they believe God is leading the church to do often find that their excitement rubs off on the donors with whom they have contact. If they cannot infect a congregant with exuberance about the ministry, they are not going to engage them in generous giving.

Courage

One of the most appealing aspects of great leaders is their demonstrations of courage in the act of ministry. When a leader steps out in faith, confidently proclaiming God's promises for the church, boldly challenging the people of God and aggressively taking the point on the march into the unknown, people are more likely to follow. Leaders that pursue safe, low-risk adventures will probably not incite people to be generous. Ministry that pursues that which can only be accomplished through deep conviction, sincere effort and the blessing of God inspires people to join the team.

Impact

People want their giving to count; they measure the "profitability" of their giving by how much of a difference their benevolence made in the lives of people. As a leader, do you empower your congregants to invest their limited resources in ways that enable them to make a discernible impact for Christ?

Churches whose leaders meet these standards inevitably raise more money—and raise it more easily—than do the leaders who either do not possess these abilities, or who have failed to convey the existence of those abilities to their congregation.

It is not enough these days for the senior pastor or dominant leader within the congregation to have such qualities. It is essential that whoever is charged with leading the stewardship campaign exhibit these character qualities as well. If the senior pastor is not the point person for the stewardship or fund-raising campaign—and, as mentioned earlier, the pastor should not be awarded that role—then the person who is selected must possess the leadership abilities and personal character traits that will facilitate positive emotions and expectations about the ministry.

The Lay Leadership Team

As in every leadership situation, a strong point person must be visible to those seeking direction and motivation. Many congregations have discovered, however, that although it is imperative to have a strong point person lead the stewardship effort, the campaign is likely to suffer if it is based solely or primarily upon the efforts of that point person.

The most effective fund-raising efforts are those that involve a multitude of people in a carefully conceived, well-managed campaign. The pastor or another key person may be the standard bearer for the campaign, but a team of competent and committed assistants is integral to pulling off the campaign according to plan. This requires not just identifying and enlisting people willing to engage in the process, but also empowering people to make decisions in line with the philosophy, goals and guidelines developed for the campaign.

> **THE MOST EFFECTIVE FUND-RAISING EFFORTS ARE THOSE THAT INVOLVE A MULTITUDE OF PEOPLE IN A CAREFULLY CONCEIVED, WELL-MANAGED CAMPAIGN.**

Again, the issue of leadership is crucial. Who will lead the stewardship team?

Only one out of every five pastors who serves at a church that utilizes a lay team for fund-raising actually retains the primary leadership role within that team. In those churches, the pastor typically appoints or assembles the team, provides guidance and creative input and issues final approval of plans and proposals in consideration of the church's vision, doctrine, theology and policies. The pastors who are most likely to retain leadership of the process are those serving small churches (particularly those that have fewer than 50 people in attendance a week) and those pastoring working-class congregations. Pastors of large or more affluent church bodies generally delegate such authority and responsibility to lay leaders and serve primarily as the final stamp of approval.

Selecting the team members usually happens in one of two ways. The traditional approach, as noted, is for the senior pastor to invite a group of trusted people to be part of the team. This is the approach of nearly 6 out of 10 churches that have a stewardship campaign, regardless of whether or not the pastor then provides the operational leadership to the group. The benefit of this strategy is that it ensures the pastor of a person with whom he can work comfortably, and one whose values are likely to reflect those of the church and its pastor. This selection method maximizes the comfort level of the pastor, but it may not result in the most effective possible campaign.

An increasingly common strategy is for the pastor or senior leadership team of the church to select the director of the campaign. Once that person accepts the position and its attendant responsibilities, the director's first act is to identify, recruit and mobilize a team of his or her choosing. This process furthers the stewardship director's sense of ownership and empowerment and prevents mid-campaign or post-campaign excuses such as, "It's the best I can do with the team I inherited."

Theoretically, the more responsibility and authority that can be delegated to the congregants, the better off the church will be in its fund-raising ventures. This fits the concept of autonomous work teams, which has been widely embraced in businesses, nonprofit organizations as well as some churches during the past several years. Does the concept work in the context of church fund-raising? Moderately well, according to pastors.

Four out of 10 pastors say their teams have been very effective; half say they have been somewhat effective; just 1 out of 10 says the money-raising teams have not been effective. Often the struggles experienced by the team had more to do with church politics, the mind-set of the congregation regarding money and financial duties, and the failure of the church to adequately equip the lay team for its responsibilities than with the inherent inability of a lay team to satisfactorily conceive, plan and implement a stewardship campaign.

Full Disclosure

As an aside, I was intrigued to learn that in almost half of all Protestant churches (44 percent) the senior pastor has unrestricted access to the giving activity and history of people within his church. Perhaps more importantly, though, I found that such access is most common in the churches that are most effective in stewardship activity.

Often the fear is that if pastors have knowledge of how much money specific individuals or families donate to the church, then those individuals will be treated differently or inappropriately (i.e., with undue favor or neglect). I was pleased to find, however, little evidence of abuse of such information. Few pastors make personal requests of the most generous donors when a particular need arises within the church. Only 8 percent of all senior pastors initiate contact with large donors in the congregation, even on an occasional basis, in the hope of receiving a special donation to pay for a special or immediate need.

As some of the pastors we interviewed pointed out, the danger is not so much in treating people differently as in treating people unfairly. Regardless of what they donate to the church, everyone gets treated differently; the real danger is in responding to people in an unfair manner simply because of their stewardship practices.

Unequal treatment is an unavoidable human tendency, and generally is an appropriate tendency. The Bible is filled with examples of leaders treating the people they led in different ways. Treating everyone the same would create massive problems, because people have different needs, circumstances, expectations and reactions. A sensitive leader absorbs and interprets reality in a manner that allows addressing each individual according to who the person is, where the person is coming from, the person's needs or wants and what is best for him or her. Different treatment is a necessity; unique responsiveness is one of the hallmarks of any wholesome relationship.

> ## IN STEWARDSHIP, TREATING PEOPLE DIFFERENTLY IS NOT THE SAME AS TREATING THEM UNFAIRLY.

Treating people unfairly, however, is inappropriate, regardless of the precipitating condition. One of the most awesome and pleasing attributes of God is His fairness to His creation. One of Jesus' core principles was that we treat each other with dignity, respect, love and compassion—the manifestations of fairness.

One pastor used the analogy of parenting as he described his justification for treating his congregants differently but with equity. A good parent knows that even though her two sons came from the same womb, each is a unique person and requires a different parental touch to mature fully. The way one child is taught, disciplined, encouraged and rewarded may be radically different from the ways these functions are handled with the other child. Allowances for personal distinctiveness must be made for the child's own good. Yet the same parent must respond to each child with fairness, no matter how different the children are, lest resentment, anger and other unhealthy responses result.

Why should a pastor risk the possibility of leading people unfairly because he is aware of how much money they give to the church? Because the pastor is generally one of the key strategists involved in the stewardship campaign and in the aggregate financial oversight of the church. Having a detailed understanding of the giving patterns within the church facilitates clearer strategic planning, even if the pastor is not the director of the campaign.

Pastors use giving data as a means of assessing how to broach the topic of financial need within the church, and how to conceive fund-raising plans for church-wide implementation. You cannot make good decisions without good information. At some point, we have to trust the professionalism of pastors and recognize that in cases where the congregation expects the pastor to be accountable for the financial condition of the church, he or she must be given the information required to do the job properly.

In many churches, the pastor includes financial performance among the aspects of lifestyle to which the individual is held accountable. Some pastors seem uncomfortable with this task and may state that it is none of their business how much money a congregant gives: "That is between the donor and the Lord." But why is the line of accountability drawn on this issue and not on others? If a person has made a commitment to Christ and to His church, doesn't that individual then accept the church as an accountability partner?

What kind of message does the church send to its people when it teaches that we are accountable for all of our actions, and when we strive to help people remain true to biblical principles in all areas of life—except the financial realm? To the pastors of many churches this seems inconsistent, implying that money is somehow too sensitive or sacred a resource for the church to monitor. An old axiom says: "Money is a good servant but a poor master." By denying the church a role in helping people practice stewardship fully, we seem to make money a master rather than a servant.

Good Financial Management

Strong leadership may clear the way for people to consider giving generously. That leadership, though, may not be enough. You must also wipe out any doubts or fears they may have regarding the ability of the church to manage its money effectively. This is best done, of course, by exposing the people to a track record of excellent financial decisions. In the eyes of many donors, the best predictor of future behavior is likely to be past behavior: Your history of stellar financial performance may be your best argument for why they should trust you with their money in the future.

> **THE SOONER YOU ESTABLISH A TRACK RECORD OF SUPERB FINANCIAL PERFORMANCE, THE SOONER PEOPLE WILL TRUST YOU WITH THEIR MONEY.**

People need to know more, though, than the fact that the church's revenues and expenses balanced at the end of the fiscal year. The following is some of the information that heightens people's confidence.

Budgets
Budgets are more than simply a routine planning practice that help organi-

zations manage money. They are a means of identifying priorities. They become a symbol of the depth and quality of forethought invested in the ministry. Budgets operate as a guide to effective resource allocation and an arbiter of conflict. Just as important as these operational realities, however, is the role budgets play in building people's confidence in the church. Take budgeting seriously. Use the process itself as a signal of professionalism. As you minister effectively, within budget, use that capacity as a further sign that the church is effective at managing people's investments.

Quality Controls

When your people examine how the church handles its money, what do they see? What kinds of safeguards, checks and balances are in place? For example, think about the money collected from offerings at worship services or other public events. What happens to money from the time it leaves a donor's hand to the time it winds up in the church's bank account? Who are the servants charged with collecting the funds? Where is the money stored once it has been collected? Who counts it—and how many people are present at that time? What kind of accountability procedures exist? Who deposits the cash in the bank, and who checks the veracity of those deposits?

Congregants observe the little things and translate those observations to all the practices they assume take place in the church. How much scrutiny do you assign to this avenue of your ministry? Your people should feel confident that satisfactory quality control systems help to manage the flow of money.

Expertise

Your church does not need a team of certified public accountants as its stewardship team. However, the people chosen to handle the financial decisions and to institute the financial practices of the church should impress the congregation. They impress them not with MBAs or fancy titles from the world of finance (although that can help!), but through evidence of common sense, monetary savvy and unblemished integrity. The church should be open to hiring external expertise on an as-needed basis to further raise the congregation's comfort level of church financial management.

Access

Every child knows that the moment you deny him or her access to something, that entity contains something of special interest or importance. It is the same with church finances. Deny congregants access to information about church income and church spending and the automatic assumption is that dark secrets are being hidden. Mischief, skeletons in the closet, mismanagement, extortion—all kinds of assumptions and gossip may emerge when the church says that the very people who gave the money have forfeited the right to know what happened to it once they handed it over to "their" church.

We discovered that churches that have a policy of open access to all financial information (except data regarding how much money specific people have given) experience fewer financial disputes and accusations than do churches that maintain those records under strict security. When the church has a policy—and an attitude—of openness about its finances, people's skepticism is held in check.

You may be interested to know, incidentally, that in more than a decade of studying how donors examine the financial practices of churches, it is extremely rare for people who donate to a church having an "open books" policy to actually request to see the financial records. In most cases, simply knowing they have such access communicates much more to them than they would glean from hours of time spent poring over those records. Giving people the ability to ask questions and to receive nondefensive answers, without indignation about raising those questions, is invaluable to the health of the church.

Audits

Amazingly, in no other segment of the nonprofit marketplace are the financial controls as lax as in those that characterize Christian churches. A large majority of nonreligious nonprofit entities pay for an independent financial audit of their records every year. It has become standard operating procedure.

In our research, however, we were shocked to discover that less than one out of every five Protestant churches hires an accounting firm to evaluate the church's financial condition and practices. Interestingly, among the churches that use audits, the pastors typically indicated two primary benefits of those audits.

First, the church gained invaluable insight into its financial standing and potential. Because the accountants have no vested interest in the church, they provide objective expertise that helps the church itself become a better steward of people's investment in the ministry.

Second, the image conveyed to the public by having an audit more than pays for the expense of the practice. Providing a statement from a recognized, reputable accounting firm indicating that the church's finances live up to the accepted standards of the accounting industry can buy the church a lot of credibility.

In short, the more thoroughly people's doubts, fears and questions can be dismissed by strategic financial activities such as those listed here, the more likely the church is to raise a solid donor base.

Model the Expected Behavior

Finally, leaders are most effective when they practice what they preach. People learn best by watching others and imitating what they see. When it comes to fund-raising, adults are more likely to give to an organization when they see that the key leaders—those who are on the inside and know just how effective the organization really is—are ardently supporting the work of the church.

Confidentiality is an important element in fund-raising, so informing the Body of the specific financial gifts given by the leaders of the church must be handled carefully.

Often a fund-raising period is kicked off by letting the congregation know the aggregate pledges and commitments of the staff and elders (or other lay leaders) as an indication of the level of support the "diehards" are showing toward the ministry. This must be handled deftly, of course; if the leaders do not give evidence of being deeply committed to the ministry through their giving, then the rest of the people will follow that cue and give meagerly. If, however, the leaders are enthusiastic about the church and are willing to fervently support what the church is attempting to do, then the congregation at large is more likely to catch the spirit and follow that lead.

> **YOU CANNOT REASONABLY EXPECT THE CONGRE-GATION TO MAKE A WHOLEHEARTED FINANCIAL COMMITMENT TO THE CHURCH IF THE LEADERS OF THE CHURCH DO NOT SOMEHOW REFLECT THAT SAME DEPTH OF COMMITMENT.**

One insight that emerged from the research is that many pastors fail to provide adequate modeling of effective stewardship. Some pastors believe that because they do not make as much money as many in their congregations, they do not have to give generously or sacrificially to the church. I encountered others who saw themselves as spiritual leaders and thus thought their giving was of no special interest to the church. A few others stated that they do not have to give as much money to the church because they donate an extraordinary amount of time to the ministry. Fortunately, these pastors are a small minority of the Body of church leaders.

The congregation need not know how much money the pastor or staff give to the church. It is probably not good for them to have specific details in this regard. The church typically benefits, though, by intentionally providing for the congregation clear indications that their spiritual leaders *believe* in stewardship and *practice* the very principles they teach to the congregation. No person is above the principles of God, whether those principles relate to finances or other aspects of lifestyle. Make no mistake about it: The way the pastor responds to the call to give sets the tone for the church.

chapter

11

Challenges to Churches

> "THERE ARE THREE IRREFUTABLE RULES
> WHICH WILL ASSURE YOUR SUCCESS IN
> FUNDRAISING. UNFORTUNATELY, NO ONE HAS
> EVER DISCOVERED WHAT THEY ARE."
> JOHN RUSSELL

As a closing chapter, let me offer a summary of some key principles for effective stewardship. Our challenge is to create an environment and facilitate a mind-set in which people want to donate money to the church for the right reasons. The following are some guidelines toward achieving that outcome.

1. **You are raising money for life transformation, not organizational survival.**

Your objective must be to advance the cause of ministry, not to perpetuate the survival of an institution. God can make great things happen in people's lives without an organization through which such ministry happens. Focus on the essential: seeing lives changed for the glory and purposes of God.

2. **People give to people and causes, not to institutions or programs.**

If you want to inspire people to become good stewards, help them see themselves as ministers. Their giving is a means of using their resources for the very reason they exist: to know, love and serve God with all their hearts, minds, souls and strength. The way that service is manifested is by helping people. Encourage people to give to the church because it provides opportunities and means of helping people. Never forget that even if you believe church-based programs and ministries need to be funded, they only require such support because they affect people's lives. Programs and organizations are a means to an end; the end is people becoming more Christlike.

3. Repeat donors must be both inspired and persuaded.

Great fund-raisers know how to identify the soft spot that inspires people to give generously. Eliciting such support is more than just finding a "hot button"; it entails penetrating both the head and the heart of the donor. If you want a person to give you a one-time donation, he or she can be persuaded through a momentary tug on the heart strings, or through a compelling and irrefutable argument. Your goal, though, should be to create a stewardship mind-set. You do not want to have to start from scratch every time you need money; you want to build on a foundation you have worked hard to develop, one that is based on trust, integrity and mutual benefit. In developing the stewardship mentality, provide prospective supporters with both inspiration and persuasion—a one-two knockout punch that reaps lasting results by inciting commitment.

4. There is no substitute for absolute integrity. None.

Honesty, transparency, accessibility—these are the characteristics on which a great stewardship campaign—and genuine, life changing ministry—are based. Integrity is not something to be fooled with: Lose it and you will pay a major price for an extended period. Often, once the people's trust has been violated, the relationship cannot be restored until many years have passed and the donors who were hurt by the infraction are gone. Many ministries cannot outlast that era. As servants of the church, we have a sacred trust with the people in the congregation; as ambassadors of Christ we have an awesome privilege and responsibility to represent Him and His cause. Never entertain practices or teachings that are of a dubious ethical nature. Take the high road. It is the only route available to pleasing the One for whom we ultimately raise funds.

5. A visionless church is an impoverished church.

Many pastors recognize that God has gifted them to teach, but they are best at communicating information and challenges rather than inspiration. That is one reason it is so important to know and repeatedly articulate God's vision for the church to the people. Can you imagine your peers in the church receiving God's vision for the future He wants them to establish and *not* feeling motivated to serve beyond their natural ability? Besides the many practical and spiritual benefits to the congregation of knowing His vision, keeping the vision before the people will aid them in growing into good stewardship.

6. People give to winners; tell your stories.

Effective ministries are balanced ministries. In fund-raising, your church must maintain an appropriate balance between humility and pride. When God works through your church to accomplish great things, the people need to know of God's deeds. We can take a measure of pride in the fact that we were available, we were useful and we played a role in bestowing blessings from Him upon people who needed His touch. We must simultaneously remember that it is His accomplishment, not ours. In a spirit of humility and awe, we must convey the truth of His works in our midst. Allow people the pleasure of acknowledging His presence, His caring and His partnership with us. Such knowledge goes much farther in encouraging a lifestyle of stewardship than do a hundred fund-raising gimmicks. People want to connect with God! Make it easy for them to do so.

7. Fund-raising is a means to an end. Focusing on the end facilitates the means.

Do not let the process overshadow the product. We raise money not for operations, institutions or tradition, but for ministry. People can get cynical, fatigued and upset when you keep sounding the call for money—unless the focus is not on the object of the request (i.e., money) but on the outcome of the response (i.e., ministry).

8. Dream big, pray big, ask big, minister big.

No dream, no vision, no need, no ministry transcends the capacity of our God. Sometimes we reflect our lack of faith in our unwillingness to let Him determine the vision, and in our refusal to truly believe He can accomplish incredible things through us. Our research consistently shows that people set their own sights based on the expectations placed upon them by the people and institutions they trust: Set your expectations low and people will never surprise you. As a leader in your church, take your cues from God and show your confidence in Him through the boldness of your plans, your confidence, your requests and your ministry. He never fails Himself; get in touch with His vision, His will and His calling for you and your church, and hold on for the ride of your life. Resources will be the least of your problems.

9. Ministry donors do not just give; they invest.

Set your sights high. Challenge people to do their homework, to evaluate all the options they have for stewardship and to behave as wise investors of funds. Once your investors have done their part, live up to your part of the bargain: Give them an unbeatable return on the investment. As in the stock market, when you allow them to multiply their investment, they will continue to invest in you. Lead the church in such a way that it proves their investment is an act of discernment, not an act of foolishness.

10. Stewardship is a lifestyle, not an event.

You may choose to sponsor fund-raising events, but always remind your people that *stewardship* is a way of living. As in every dimension of our lives, if we take God's promises and admonitions seriously, and develop habits that reflect those promises and admonitions, we will soon be able to transfer our focus from wondering if He will bless us for our faithfulness to amazement at how He blesses us. Encouraging Christians to recognize stewardship as a 24-hour-a-day, 7-days-a-week mentality is a core objective in any stewardship campaign. Encouraging them to incorporate all our God-given resources into this lifestyle of obedience will revolutionize the environment at your church, as well as the lives of your congregants.

11. Listen carefully, respond strategically, thank people sincerely.

Good leaders listen to the people; they respond to what they hear in strategic ways, and when the people live up to the expectations placed upon them, sincere appreciation is one of the rewards and ongoing motivations for their continued involvement. Just as people give for the benefit of other people, so they also give in response to those who have demonstrated sufficient interest and concern about the donor to spark such generosity. The Holy Spirit gets the credit for inspiring people to give; and you must allow the Holy Spirit to direct your steps, too, as you interact with your donors.

12. Use the pastor appropriately in the stewardship process.

The pastor has been called as the spiritual leader of the church. Although stewardship is one of the spiritual endeavors the people must understand, embrace and live out, the pastor should not be the chief fundraiser. That undermines the pastor's standing in the eyes of the people. The pastor must embrace the stewardship process, model it, teach it, help strategically prepare the stewardship campaign and publicly and unabashedly endorse the campaign. The church does the pastor—and the congregation—a disservice if it expects the pastor to be the primary fund-raiser.

13. People appreciate useful information.

Do not shy away from opportunities to teach your congregation about the joys, challenges and privilege of being God's stewards. If taught in a practical, sensitive and Bible-based manner, people are grateful for information that helps them know and fulfill their responsibilities as believers. Most Christians are pleased to discover that we are stewards, not mere consumers; that we have an obligation to the church that supports us spiritually; that we are to invest, not just give away our money; and that we are stewards of more than just money.

14. Let love, compassion and servanthood—not dollar goals—be your motivations.

It is incredibly easy to get caught up in "the chase" and forget the purpose of a stewardship campaign. It is not about meeting goals. It is not about raising money. It is not about beating last year's totals, or outraising other churches. Your campaign is about ministering to your people so they can minister to others and receive the joy of obedience and servanthood. Model that attitude for them. It is contagious.

> **May God grant you the vision, the wisdom, the talent and the opportunities to raise up a congregation of people committed to demonstrating their love for Christ and their commitment to His cause through their insistence upon serving as worthy stewards of His resources.**

Appendices

appendix

1

Data Tables from Survey Research

Table 1

CHURCH DONOR DEMOGRAPHICS
(N=1015)

Characteristic	Gave to a church in the past 12 months:	
	Yes	No
Median age (in years)	44	37
Gross household income ($000)	33.3	24.3
Graduated from college	24%	19%
Currently married	69	51
Have ever been divorced	18	21
Have kids under 18 in the household	40	45
Ethnic group: white	81	66
Registered voter	85	75
Ideologically conservative	36	22
Gender: male	45	52

Source: OmniPoll™ 2-94, July 1994; Barna Research Group Ltd., Oxnard, CA.

Table 2

SELF-PERCEPTIONS BY DONOR STATUS AND CHURCH ATTENDANCE
(N=1015)

Self-perception	Church donor?		Attend church, but not a donor
	Yes	No	
Happy	98%	92%	91%
Excited about life	89	82	82
Religious	88	60	83
Born-again Christian*	62	35	41
Too busy	47	47	57
Stressed out	23	27	17
Superstitious	14	20	18
Wealthy	6	5	11
Lonely	5	7	14

*The term "born-again Christian" was provided as one of the adjectives for respondents to either accept or reject as an accurate description of themselves. Throughout our research and reporting, however, we do not use this measure to classify people as born-again Christians. Instead, we rely upon two questions that we ask of all respondents—questions that do not include the terminology "born-again Christian." See footnote 4 in chapter 1 for a description of how we define born-again Christians in our research and how the term is used throughout this book.

Source: OmniPoll™ 2-94, July 1994; Barna Research Group Ltd., Oxnard, CA.

Table 3

LIFE OUTCOMES DEEMED VERY DESIRABLE
(N=1202)

Life outcome or condition	Church donor? Yes	No	Attend church, but not a donor
Points of differentiation:			
Close relationship with God	87%	66%	74%
Clear purpose for life	87	76	81
Close, personal friendships	86	74	71
Being part of a local church	71	35	54
Influencing others' lives	48	33	41
Points of similarity:			
Good health	90%	93%	98%
Comfortable lifestyle	73	72	87
Live close to family	65	62	65
Live to an old age	54	58	61
Active sex life	50	52	42
High-paying job	38	47	48
Own a large home	26	32	34
Achieve fame or public recognition	9	10	15

Source: OmniPoll™ 2-93, July 1993; Barna Research Group Ltd., Oxnard, CA.

— Table 4 —

DISTINCTIONS REGARDING
RELATIONSHIPS AND PEOPLE

Perspective	Church donor?	
	Yes	No
The important thing in a relationship is not how much time you spend together, but the quality of the time spent together	88%	92%
If the traditional family falls apart, American society will collapse	78	61
It is getting harder and harder to make lasting friendships	52	61
You cannot trust anyone other than family and close friends	27	20

Source: Barna Research Group Ltd., Oxnard, CA; from surveys in 1994 and 1995.

— Table 5 —

DIFFERENCES AND SIMILARITIES
REGARDING MORALS AND VALUES

Perspective	Church donor?	
	Yes	No
Abortion is morally wrong	67%	53%
Homosexuality is immoral	64	48
To get by in life these days, sometimes you have to bend the rules for your own benefit	36	56
Lying is sometimes necessary	33	37
It's almost impossible to be a moral person these days	26	34
Moral and ethical standards are as high as ever these days	17	14

Source: Barna Research Group Ltd., Oxnard, CA; from surveys in 1994, 1995 and 1996.

Table 6

ADULTS REJECT ABSOLUTE TRUTH

Perspective	Church donor? Yes	No
When it comes to morals and ethics, or what is right or wrong, there are no absolute standards that apply to everybody in all situations	65%	76%
There is no such thing as absolute truth	62	78
Nothing can be known for certain except the things you experience in your own life	53	63

Source: Barna Research Group Ltd., Oxnard, CA; from surveys in 1994, 1995 and 1996.

Table 7

ISSUES OF LIFESTYLE AND QUALITY OF LIFE

Perspective	Church donor? Yes	No
You, personally, have a responsibility to share what you have with others who are poor or struggling	94%	84%
One person can make a difference	75	70
Life is too complex these days	64	64
Main purpose in life is enjoyment and personal fulfillment	54	66
Today's children have a bright future to look forward to	41	43
Freedom means being able to do anything you want	32	30
It is better to devote yourself to following the traditional way than to pursuing your dreams	30	38
Sometimes you feel like life is not worth living	13	21

Source: Barna Research Group Ltd., Oxnard, CA; from surveys in 1994, 1995 and 1996.

Table 8

DIFFERENT VIEWS ON RELIGION
IMPACT PEOPLE'S GIVING PATTERNS

Perspective	Church donor?		Attend, do not donate
	Yes	No	
In times of crisis, you are absolutely certain that you can count on God to take care of you	93%	78%	88%
The Christian faith is relevant to the way you live today	90	73	72
It is important to be a member of a church	89	68	83
The Christian churches in your area are relevant to the way you live today	82	67	73
The Christian faith has all the answers to leading a successful life	51	37	47
No religious faith has all the answers to life's questions and challenges	51	64	53
Most churches are more interested in raising money than they are in helping people	42	53	55
A person can lead a full and satisfying life even if the person does not pursue spiritual development	34	58	39
What you do for other people is more important than what you believe about Jesus Christ	29	33	34
People's prayers do not have the power to change their circumstances	20	26	22
The whole idea of sin is outdated	13	23	19
The Ten Commandments are not relevant for people living today	11	22	20

Source: Barna Research Group Ltd., Oxnard, CA; from surveys in 1994, 1995 and 1996.

Table 9

DONORS ARE MORE LIKELY TO HAVE
EXPOSURE TO CHRISTIAN MEDIA
(N=1204)

Type of Christian message/medium	Church donor?	
	Yes	No
Read from the Bible (other than at church)	52%	26%
Watched Christian television	39	31
Listened to Christian teaching on radio	34	21
Read a Christian book	36	20
Listened to a Christian music station	28	17
Read a Christian magazine	34	13

Source: OmniPoll™ 1-94, January 1994; Barna Research Group Ltd., Oxnard, CA.

Table 10

VIEWS RELATED TO THE BIBLE
AND ITS TEACHINGS

Views regarding the Bible	Church donor?		Attend, don't donate
	Yes	No	
Percent who agreed:			
All of the miracles described in the Bible actually took place	81%	56%	86%
The Bible is absolutely accurate, and everything in it can be taken literally	61	34	39
The Bible is totally accurate in all that it teaches	52	28	53
Jesus Christ was related to King David	47	27	41
Percent who disagreed:			
The name of Noah's wife was Joan of Arc	78%	66%	69%
Jesus Christ never married because He was a priest, and priests did not marry	64	50	55
All religious faiths teach equally valid truths	57	51	65
One of the books of the New Testament is the Book of Thomas, written by the apostle Thomas	54	36	45
The entire Bible was written several decades after Jesus' death and resurrection	45	34	36
The Bible teaches that money is the root of all evil	44	32	41

Source: Barna Research Group Ltd., Oxnard, CA; from surveys in 1994, 1995 and 1996.

Table 11

BELIEFS ABOUT DEITY VARY

Views regarding the Trinity/deity	Church donor?		Attend, don't donate
	Yes	No	
There is a god who hears people's prayers and has the power to answer those prayers	95%	79%	91%
Jesus Christ was a real person	93	82	86
Jesus Christ was born to a virgin	94	66	93
Jesus Christ rose from the dead and is spiritually alive today	91	69	82
Jesus will come back	82	57	73
God is the all-powerful, all-knowing, perfect Creator of the universe who rules the world today	80	57	69
Satan was at one time an angel who served God in heaven	77	62	74
Satan, or the devil, is not a living being but is a symbol of evil	55	65	58
All people pray to the same god or spirit, no matter what name they use for that spiritual being	49	34	49
Jesus Christ sometimes made mistakes	35	54	50
When He lived on earth, Jesus Christ was human and committed sins, like other people	29	53	33

Source: Barna Research Group Ltd., Oxnard, CA; from surveys in 1994, 1995 and 1996.

Table 12

VIEWS ON SALVATION AND FORGIVENESS

Views regarding salvation	Church donor? Yes	No	Attend, don't give
Eventually, all people will be personally judged by God	94%	79%	91%
Forgiveness of sins is possible only through faith in Jesus Christ	85	55	77
People who do not consciously accept Jesus Christ as their Savior will be condemned to hell	54	28	38
If a person is generally good, or does enough good things for others during life, the person will earn a place in heaven	45	61	52
All people will experience the same outcome after death, regardless of their religious beliefs	44	48	37
All good people, whether or not they consider Jesus Christ to be their Savior, will live in heaven after they die on earth	40	50	48
There are some crimes, sins and other things people might do that cannot be forgiven by God	24	38	39

Source: Barna Research Group Ltd., Oxnard, CA; from surveys in 1994, 1995 and 1996.

Table 13

PERSPECTIVES ON SUPERNATURAL POWER

Views regarding power	Church donor? Yes	Church donor? No	Attend, but don't give
Prayer can change what happens in life	94%	71%	84%
God's Holy Spirit lives within people who have accepted Jesus Christ as their Savior	90	65	88
Tarot cards are a reliable source of guidance for life decisions	8	10	5
Crystals can provide supernatural power	8	6	2
Astrology can accurately predict the future	7	9	9

Source: Barna Research Group Ltd., Oxnard, CA; from surveys in 1994, 1995 and 1996.

Table 14

Why People Give to Nonprofit Organizations
(N=1164)

Reason for giving	Accuracy of this description			
	Very	Some-what	Not too	Not at all
They have a great reputation for being reliable and trustworthy	66%	27%	2%	4%
You feel good about yourself when you know that you have helped others	59	31	5	6
The organization is involved in a type of work that is of great interest to you	54	35	4	4
You have seen or studied the work of the organization firsthand and know they're trustworthy	49	36	4	9
The organization is highly recommended by people you know personally and trust	39	35	11	13
The organization has helped you, or people important to you, in the past	34	35	10	20
The organization serves people in a geographic area that is of interest to you	31	40	13	14
The organization has made donating to them easy and simple	30	38	12	18
The organization is highly rated by groups that study the work of nonprofit organizations	27	39	13	17
You were particularly moved by an appeal they made	20	41	17	20
You attended an event sponsored by the organization and were impressed	19	33	17	29
You receive a tax deduction	14	25	21	40
You expect the organization to provide you with some type of help or service in the future	12	16	19	51
A celebrity or personality whom you respect is promoting the organization	8	15	19	56
The organization is offering a gift or other itemof interest to you in return for a modest donation	4	10	15	69

Source: OmniPoll™ 4-94, November 1994; Barna Research Group Ltd., Oxnard, CA.

Table 15

BORN-AGAIN CHRISTIANS PREFER GIVING TO DIFFERENT TYPES OF ORGANIZATIONS

Type of organization	Born-again Christian? Yes	No
Handicapped assistance	68%	72%
Health care, medical	43	45
Religious (exclude churches)	42	22
Local community development	35	36
Colleges, educational	32	36
Wildlife, environmental	25	43
Music, arts, cultural	20	26
Public policy, PACs	19	24
International relief/development	19	21
Political parties	16	21
Subgroup size	453	711

Source: OmniPoll™ 4-94, November 1994; Barna Research Group Ltd., Oxnard, CA.

Table 16

BORN-AGAIN CHRISTIANS GIVE TO THE LEFT, BUT THEY ARE MORE LIKELY TO GIVE TO THE RIGHT

Organization supported	Born-again Christian? Yes	No
Focus on the Family	18%	3%
National Rifle Association	18	15
Christian Coalition	11	3
Operation Rescue	10	6
Planned Parenthood	9	19
National Organization for Women	5	14
People for the American Way	3	3
American Civil Liberties Union	2	7

Source: OmniPoll™ 4-94, November 1994; Barna Research Group Ltd., Oxnard, CA.

Table 17

EVANGELICAL CHRISTIANS PREFER
DIFFERENT TYPES OF ORGANIZATIONS

Type of organization	Evangelical Christian? Yes	No
Religious (exclude churches)	74%	25%
Handicapped assistance	65	71
Health care, medical	40	45
Local community development	38	36
Colleges, educational	38	34
Public policy, PACs	27	22
International relief/development	25	20
Wildlife, environmental	19	38
Political parties	16	19
Music, arts, cultural	12	24
Subgroup size	106	1058

Source: OmniPoll™ 4-94, November 1994; Barna Research Group Ltd., Oxnard, CA.

Table 18

WHAT DOES A RELATIONSHIP WITH A CHARITABLE ORGANIZATION LOOK LIKE?
(N=527)

Description of the relationship	Donor's age group:				Religious associations:		
	18-29	30-49	50-64	65+	Evang.	Prot.	Cath.
Member/director/ volunteer	16%	35%	25%	27%	33%	32%	17%
Have shared goals, ideas; worthwhile cause	18	17	27	19	21	21	14
It's a positive relationship	20	16	24	17	18	20	12
Helped donor, friends, family	16	15	15	23	12	17	22
Feel close/ connected to them	9	9	12	8	11	9	11
Feel informed, but detached	18	11	5	14	16	11	9
Feel involved/ part of them	11	9	6	8	7	8	9
Feel good about giving/feel needed	5	4	7	9	4	5	6
Appreciate their work	2	4	4	6	5	5	6
Cordial, friendly; personal ties	7	3	3	4	9	4	3
Good cause; can see the results	9	4	4	3	7	4	4
Aware of organization's needs	4	3	6	3	0	2	7
Personal need for their help	0	3	3	1	4	3	3
Give them money	5	2	2	6	0	3	1

Source: OmniPoll™ 4-94, November 1994; Barna Research Group Ltd., Oxnard, CA.

Table 19

INTEREST IN DIFFERENT TYPES OF EVENTS
(N=479)

How likely to attend	Definitely	Probably	Prob. not	Definitely not
Hear people helped by the NPO speak about their experience	13%	50%	31%	5%
Fund-raiser with top-rate entertainment and with speaker from NPO	12	56	25	6
Large gathering of supporters where NPO reps listen to supporter concerns, ideas	12	52	28	6
Informal dinner with NPO leaders	12	48	31	7
Satellite broadcast to centers around the nation to update supporters	5	30	50	15
Dessert, house party for area supporters	7	40	43	10

Source: OmniPoll™ 4-94, November 1994; Barna Research Group Ltd., Oxnard, CA.

Table 20

TYPES OF NONCHURCH MINISTRIES
SUPPORTED BY DONORS

(PERCENT OF DONORS WHO GAVE TO
ANY PARACHURCH MINISTRY)

Missionaries, international missions	61%
Youth ministry	45
Social welfare ministry	38
Discipleship ministry	33
Christian education ministry	32
Christian-based child sponsorship	32
Evangelistic ministry	29
Christian radio ministry	17
Christian television ministry	15
Legal/public policy ministry	11

Source: OmniPoll™ 1-96, January 1996; Barna Research Group Ltd., Oxnard, CA.

Table 21

THE OLDER PEOPLE ARE, THE MORE
LIKELY THEY ARE TO DONATE TO CHURCH

Baby busters (18 to 32 years old)	31%
Baby boomers (33 to 51 years old)	43
Builders (52 to 69 years old)	54
Seniors (70 or older)	61

Source: Two surveys conducted by Barna Research Group Ltd., Oxnard, CA, in 1996;
N=2022.

Table 22

CHURCH GIVING VARIES BY AFFILIATIONS
(PERCENT OF PEOPLE FROM EACH SEGMENT WHO DONATE TO A CHURCH IN A TYPICAL MONTH)

Evangelical Christians	85%
Born-again Christians	64
Attend a Baptist church	55
Attend a Catholic church	54
Attend a Methodist church	49
Attend a charismatic church	57
Attend a mainline church	47

Source: Two surveys conducted by Barna Research Group Ltd., Oxnard, CA, in 1996; N=2022.

Table 23

WHAT CHURCHES DO TO FACILITATE FUND-RAISING

(BASE: SENIOR PASTORS OF PROTESTANT CHURCHES) (N=601)

Activity	All	Annual church budget		
		Under $100k	$100-$199k	$200k plus
Make balance sheets and other financial documents available to the congregation	94%	94%	98%	98%
Inform the congregation of the salaries of church ministers and staff people	92	94	95	90
Send people receipts at the end of the year to review how much they donated	88	84	93	97
Provide envelopes for people to insert their offering money	84	79	92	92
Publish the previous week's revenue in Sunday bulletin	45	44	52	51
Raise money from wills, trusts, estates or other legacies left to the church by members	43	39	48	59
Tell visitors not to feel obligated to give money when the offering is taken	24	22	29	25
Hire an independent accounting firm to audit the church's books	20	11	21	36
Estimate the household wealth or total giving potential of your church based on community demographic data	16	14	21	20
Require the church's departments or ministry programs to raise their own budgets	9	12	6	5
Sell books and other resources at a church bookstore or book table	9	8	12	12
Sell clothing with the church's name or logo, to raise money	5	3	7	10

Source: OmniPoll™ 3-94, April 1994; Barna Research Group Ltd., Oxnard, CA.

2

Bibliography

Callahan, Kennon. *Giving and Stewardship in an Effective Church*. San Francisco: HarperCollins, 1992.

Christian Stewardship Association. *Stewardship Resource Manual*. Milwaukee, Wis.: Christian Stewardship Association, n/d.

Getz, Gene. *A Biblical Theology of Material Possessions*. Chicago: Moody Press, 1990.

Grimm, Eugene. *Generous People*. Nashville: Abingdon Press, 1992.

Joiner, Donald, and Norma Wimberly. *The Abingdon Guide to Funding Ministry*. Nashville: Abingdon Press, 1996.

Schneider, John. *Godly Materialism*. Downers Grove, Ill.: InterVarsity Press, 1994.

Willmer, Wesley, ed. *Money for Ministries*. Wheaton, Ill.: Victor Books, 1989.

3

About George Barna and the Barna Research Group, Ltd.

George Barna is the president of the Barna Research Group, Ltd., a marketing research company located in Oxnard, California. The company specializes in conducting primary research for Christian ministries and nonprofit organizations. The vision of the Barna Research Group is to provide current, accurate and reliable information in bite-size pieces to Christian ministries in the United States, at economical costs, to enable ministry leaders to make more strategic decisions.

Since its inception in 1984, Barna Research has served more than 100 ministries, including the Billy Graham Evangelistic Association, American Bible Society, World Vision, Word Books, Thomas Nelson Publishers, Tyndale House, CBN, the Salvation Army, Willow Creek Community Church and Campus Crusade for Christ. Other nonprofit clients have included CARE, Boys and Girls Clubs, the U.S. Army, KidsPeace and United Cerebral Palsy. For-profit clients have ranged from The Disney Channel and Southwestern Bell Telephone to Prudential, Ford Motor Company and Visa.

Barna has written more than 20 books, including best-sellers such as *The Frog in the Kettle*, *User Friendly Churches*, *The Power of Vision* and *Evangelism That Works*. He is the senior editor of a bimonthly newsletter, *The Barna Report*. Several of his books have received national awards, and he is the featured presenter in two videotaped series, *The Leading Edge* series (eight topical, hour-long sessions) and *The Church in a Changing Culture* series (five sessions). He has also written more than five dozen articles for periodicals and two dozen syndicated reports based on his research.

A frequent speaker at Christian conferences, his company markets semi-

nars in which Barna helps pastors and church leaders address church dynamics, changes in our culture, people's felt needs and their expectations of the
church.

After graduating summa cum laude from Boston College, Barna earned
two master's degrees from Rutgers University, where he was awarded an
Eagleton Fellowship. He has managed campaigns for political candidates,
worked for major advertising and marketing research agencies, served as a
pastor at a megachurch and been a faculty member at several universities
and seminaries. He lives with his wife, Nancy, and their two daughters,
Samantha and Corban, in Southern California.

Notes

Notes

Notes

Notes

Resources for Cutting Edge Leaders

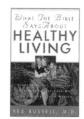

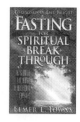

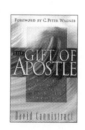
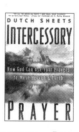

Continuing Education for Church Leaders.

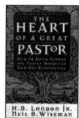

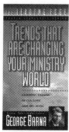

If You Liked the Book, They'll Love the Video!

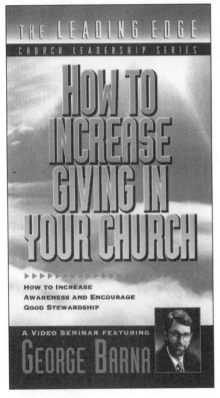

You couldn't put down the book. Now you can share it with a small group, your entire congregation or just rediscover it yourself! Video makes it easy. At last, something really worth watching on TV!

Video Benefits:

• Easily followed by any sized group

• Ideal for people who don't like to read

• Video teaches all by itself—with no need for an experienced speaker

• Fits any length training session or guest speaker time slot

• Reinforces the book's message both verbally *and* visually

Includes one video with a reproducible viewing outline.

Video • approx. 60 minutes
UPC 60135.000723

George Barna's Leading Edge Church Leadership Videos!

The Power of Vision
UPC 607135.000686
Turning Vision into Action
UPC 607135.000754
Understanding Today's Teens
UPC 607135.000709
How to Turn Around Your Church
SPCN 85116.01015

Ten Myths About Evangelism
SPCN 85116.01007
Trends that Are Changing Your Ministry World
SPCN 85116.00981
What Evangelistic Churches Do
SPCN 85116.00973

Available at your local Christian bookstore.

Gospel Light